Debrett's Guide
to
CORRESPONDENCE

by

Rolf Kurth

DEBRETT'S PEERAGE LTD

First published in 1999

By Debrett's Peerage Limited

British Library Cataloguing in Publication Data
Kurth, Rolf
Debrett's Guide to Correspondence
ISBN: 1 870 520 52 1

Printed and bound in Great Britain
by Polestar Wheatons Ltd., Exeter.

Debrett's Peerage Ltd.,
86/88 Edgware Road London W2 2YW

Rolf Kurth was born in Vancouver, Canada in 1966. After studying communications at Trinity Western University, he emigrated to Britain and served in the Royal Navy for seven years. As Flag Lieutenant (the naval equivalent of an ADC) to a senior admiral, he learned the value of observing protocol and social customs in all forms of letter writing, a skill he brings to his first book, *Debrett's Guide to Correspondence*. He finished his days in the navy as second-in-command of a warship based in Hong Kong. He is now a freelance writer and is also writing his first novel. Rolf Kurth lives in London.

Acknowledgments

It is impossible to acknowledge everybody who made this book possible. However, I would like to thank the following for their special contribution:

Murray Buesst, Esq.; Charles Burnett, Esq., Ross Herald of Arms; Mrs Helen Carter and her colleagues at the Post Office Archives & Records Service; Major Lindsay Gowland, AGC (SPS); Mrs Gerry Grattan, First Sea Lord's Office; Miss Emma Longhurst; Alexander Moncrieff, Esq.; Vice Admiral Sir Christopher Morgan, KBE; James Ricket; Mrs Mary Watson

To the residents, past and present, of No 66

Contents

Introduction 1

Chapter 1: What makes a good letter? 3

Grammar and spelling 3
Legibility 4
Clarity 5

Chapter 2: The tools of the trade 6

Stationery 6
Printing 7
Die stamp printing 8
Thermography 9
Flat printing 10
The use of heraldic devices 10
Writing paper 11
Headed writing paper 14
Correspondence cards 15
Greeting cards 20
Change of address cards 21
Envelopes 22
Addressing envelopes 23

Chapter 3: Forms of address 26

Precedence of letters 26
The use of 'Esq.' and 'Master' 31
The use of 'Ms' 32

Chapter 4: Pens and ink   33
  The signature   36
  The medium can be the message   36

Chapter 5: Topping and tailing   38
  Letter headings   38
  Beginning and ending a letter   39

Chapter 6: Invitations and replies   40
  Royal Commands   40
  Invitations by Her Majesty Queen Elizabeth The
  Queen Mother   42
  Invitations by other Members of the Royal Family .   43
  Invitations to formal events   43
  Social invitations   47
  'at Home' cards   48
    RSVP and *'pour memoir'*   52
    Letters to invite   54
    Telephone to remind?   54

Chapter 7: Marking the occasions of life   55
  Births   55
  Christening   56
  Announcing an engagement   56
  Birthday parties   57
  Wedding invitations   59
    The traditional wedding invitation   60
    Example of informal wedding invitations   62
    Replying to wedding invitations   62
  Reply cards   63
  Thankyou cards   65
  Death and letters of condolence   66
  Breaking difficult news   69

Chapter 8: The thankyou letter 71

   When should you write? 72
   To whom should you write? 72
   What should you say? 73
   Comment on appropriateness 74
   Use of humour 74
   Mention all the hosts 75
   Mention other guests 75
   Apologise for any misbehaviour 75
   Things to avoid 76
   Methods of delivery 77

Chapter 9: The begging letter 80

   Asking for favours 80
   Apologies and making up with people 80
   Renewing friendships 83
   Asking yourself to stay 83

Chapter 10: Letters of affection 86

   Letters to children 86
   Letters to lovers — when things go wrong 87

Chapter 11: The letter as a diary 89

Chapter 12: Fax and email 90

   Faxes 90
   Email 91

Chapter 13: Conducting business from home 93

   Job applications 96
   The timing of your application 97

References 102
  Asking for a reference 103
  Giving a reference 103
Resignation 104

Chapter 14: Writing to your Member of Parliament . 106

Chapter 15: Methods of delivery 109

Appendix: Correct forms of address 115

Useful addresses 120

Bibliography 120

Introduction

Is the personal handwritten letter an anachronism? Is the art of letter writing dead? In this day of the word processor, electronic mail, faxes, modems, pagers, and mobile telephones, has the letter, written with pen and ink and delivered by 'snail-mail,' had its day? Of course not. Perhaps even more so in this day of instant communication, a letter has a very powerful message and perhaps the medium gives it most of its power.

The written word had its beginnings in about 3000 BC with clay tablets and a wooden stylo or pencil. Characters began to be formalised, first in the form of pictures, or hieroglyphs, then to more advanced alphabets. The earliest European letter written on paper is credited to Raymond, Duke of Narbonne who penned a letter to King Henry III in AD 1216. The Egyptians seem to have been the first to use papyrus from around 1200 BC which was used right up until the 6th century AD by both the Greeks and Romans. Paper as we know it today was first used by the Chinese as a writing material in the 2nd century AD. Scribes were employed to write on behalf of monarchs and noblemen until writing became an occupation of the common man. Primarily since the invention of a supple medium on which to write, people have been communicating with one another using the written word. It seems somehow an integral part of our humanness to want to be heard and understood. When we are not in close proximity of those with whom we wish to communicate, we simply

1

find a way to transmit that message. Distance then seems the likely reason to write letters; however, today many of the most common of social letters are written to those nearby. We write to convey thought, to impart knowledge or to pass on a message.

In this book, I touch upon the most common letters written today. It is not solely a book about forms of address, nor is it solely about the etiquette of letter writing. In fact, it is both. My goal was to create a reference book which simplifies the art of social correspondence. Taking information from many sources, I have distilled that large pool of information into an easy to use guide to the most common of today's letters written from home.

The majority of the information you will see in this book is not new; I make no apology for that. Much of the way we write is dictated through tradition which has been developed and adapted over the past few hundred years since social letter writing came to the fore in society. Although I have taken a traditional stance, I have brought it up to date to suit most of the situations in which we find ourselves in this modern world.

* * * * * * *

Chapter 1

═══

What Makes a Good Letter?

Writing is work, and to do this work well, you have many tools at your disposal, many of which will be dealt with in the next section. To make a letter work, however, or indeed, work for you, there are certain aspects which we must get right. If, for example, you were to receive an immaculately presented letter but it was full of grammatical errors and spelling mistakes, the message might well be lost completely. So before the medium is looked at in any great detail, let us examine the nuts and bolts of letter writing.

Grammar and spelling

An in-depth examination of grammar falls outside the scope of this book, but if you know that your spelling is atrocious, have a dictionary to hand when writing, or even use a computerised spell-check program. Even when writing a social letter, which will certainly be handwritten when sent, I often draft the letter on my laptop so that I can easily edit the letter for grammatical mistakes and have the benefit of the spelling feature in the word-processing program that I use. Granted it may take a few minutes more and is perhaps a rather cumbersome way of writing, but it does allow you to produce a perfect letter before you even take the cap off your pen. If, like me, you are prone to changing syntax mid-flow, this option will negate having to rewrite a letter several times.

There are many good books available which teach grammar without going back to a textbook style of learning. They show examples of common mistakes in the English language and give useful suggestions. If you think your grammar might be in need of a polish, consider picking up one of these books and reminding yourself of all those rules you learned at school. It is interesting to note some of the changes to rules that were pummelled into us as children and also to notice how even in our own generation we can see how the English language has evolved. The fact that you are reading this book shows that you have a commitment to improving your letter writing skills; taking the time to ensure your grammar and spelling are correct will go a very long way indeed to improving your art.

Legibility

Many of us are unwilling to admit that our handwriting is atrocious. With the advent of the word processor, many of us these days hardly ever put pen to paper. We spend our days in front of a computer screen communicating by email or fax. Yet, ensuring that our handwriting is legible, is one of the keystones of pen craft; similarly with grammar and spelling, making text readable is of paramount importance. In 1990, I left university after three years of typing essays, and joined the Royal Navy. I was soon sent to sea and was forced to begin letter writing in earnest. It was only when a senior officer jokingly asked if I could do 'joined-up writing' that I realised how atrocious my handwriting actually was. With that in mind, I forced myself to sit down on a regular basis and develop a style, in the same way that many of us practised a signature in our adolescent days. I always pity my mother who received letters from a friend who shall remain nameless; my poor mother had to pass the letter around the family for each of us to have a go at deciphering the bad handwriting. So, as with anything, practice makes perfect and the time spent improving your longhand will be time well spent.

Clarity

Clarity is broadly defined as making something clear or freeing it from obscurity or impurity. In terms of letter writing, clarity is avoiding the temptation to ramble on or, in the worst case, missing the point completely. It is incredible the number of letters which are signed and posted but do not actually convey the intended message of their author. They get so bogged down in the format that they miss the point entirely. So, before even starting to put pen to paper, decide on the subject and make a quick outline of the points you wish to put across. By doing this first, you are sure to at least achieve your aim and we can then go about working on the other factors which make the letter readable and understandable.

Chapter 2

———

The Tools of the Trade

Naturally, the language of any letter is of paramount importance, yet there are many tools a writer may employ in order to make a good impression on paper. We will look here at the different types of stationery available and at the use of pens and ink.

Stationery

The choice of stationery is one of the main reasons we write. If we simply want to convey thought or pass on a message, why would we put pen to paper? In this day and age, surely it would be more expedient to send an email, fax or even telephone our recipient. By choosing to write we are given the added opportunity of expressing more of our personality through our chosen medium. To some extent the medium becomes the message. By our choice of stationery we tell our audience something of our taste, our style, and perhaps, even our means. We are given the opportunity to impress. Choosing stationery requires thought.

Printing

Before diving into the world of stationery too deeply, it would be prudent to discuss the printing process in some detail. Printing nowadays is an easily accessible service and can be fairly economical if you shop around. There are several prestige stationers who will do the printing for you as well as advise on typesetting and paper. These printers will naturally advise you on style and will help you to achieve your intended 'look'. They do not, however, come without a price. Naturally, in designing your stationery, you will need to think through what 'look' you are aiming for but you may find a printer who can give you much more help than you might first have thought. I would tend to shy away from the 'high street' chains of printers cum copying outlets which offer a very quick service. The 'look' which they so often achieve is often not the one to which you are likely to aspire.

There are a number of well known prestige stationers. Three of the most prized are the Piccolo Press in Scotland, the Wren Press in Chelsea and Smythson of Bond Street. A visit to Smythson is a must for anyone with a keen interest in stationery of all kinds. If you ask nicely, there is a very interesting little museum towards the back of their Bond Street premises which includes examples of the finest writing paper I have ever seen, printed for the Maharajas in 1920's India, complete with mother of pearl inlay and hand-painted illuminations. Whilst such extravagance is most uncommon today, Smythson's believe that "Pretty much the only thing that limits us today is the customer's imagination".

There are several methods common in printing these days, far less extravagant than those just mentioned, so I will attempt to explain each in turn.

Die stamp printing

The best quality of printing is achieved by engraving a steel die or a copperplate which is then used to die stamp the paper. This process is commonly referred to as 'engraved' printing. As the title indicates, the process of die stamping is just that, stamping. I was very lucky to have been given a rare look into the inner sanctum of the die stamp room in the basement of Smythson of Bond Street. There John Timms uses what looks like an ancient machine to die stamp each sheet of paper individually by hand. Piccolo, too, have three of these machines and they are believed to be the only ones surviving north of Manchester. The die is a block of steel which has been engraved with a crest or address; more commonly, a thin copperplate is used unless the depth of engraving requires a die, as in the case of a crest, for example. The machine inks the die or copperplate, wipes its face clean leaving ink only inside the engraved portion and then, using quite literally tons of pressure, forces the paper into the engraving. This pressure does two things: it creates what is known in the trade as blind embossing (that is, raised print devoid of ink); and, in the same process, covers the raised text in ink. This achieves what many call 'bumpy writing' with its telltale bruised appearance on the reverse of the printed surface.

Whilst this can be the most expensive method of printing for small one-off orders, if you plan to reorder subsequent runs of stationery, it is often surprisingly the most cost effective. However, if you are not living at an address where you intend to stay for a significant length of time, this may prove far too expensive. It achieves, however, the smartest and most elegant of letterheads and will always be the most correct.

Tel Symbol   01723 366798

Fax Symbol   0171-235 3844

Station Symbol

Puddleton

Figure 1: Some of the crests, monograms and devices which the Wren Press engrave for their customers.

Thermography

A popular alternative to die stamping is thermography. It is a process whereby flat, lithograph printing is sprinkled with a resin while it is still wet. The paper is then passed under ultraviolet heaters to raise the ink. It thus achieves a similar 'bumpy writing' effect, but is, even to the layman's eye, inferior in quality to die stamping. It is usually created using computerised fonts and is thus more 'perfect' than an engraved plate and loses the telltale bruising on the reverse of a die stamped piece of paper. Whilst strictly not acceptable other than for business use, economy sees it being used more and more on private stationery where small, one-off runs might be required.

Flat printing

If die stamping is not an option for financial reasons, it is far more correct and certainly preferable to use flat printing for private letterheads. Flat printing is simply lithographed text with no raised finish. It is far more economical than both die stamping and thermography and does not give the impression that one is trying to impress with what some call 'the poor man's engraving'.

The use of heraldic devices

Many people like to use what they believe is their crest on visiting cards or private stationery. It is worth noting at this point that there is no such thing as a 'family crest'. Coats of arms are granted to individuals on behalf of the Sovereign by Garter King of Arms in England and Lord Lyon in Scotland. These arms may only then be used by the direct descendants of the armigerous person by 'differencing' them using established heraldic practices. If you wish to use all or any part of the arms on a letterhead, or anything else for that matter, you must follow these strict heraldic practices. If arms were granted to one of your ancestors, you may well be entitled to use those arms (once correctly differenced), but may have to petition the College of Arms or the Court of The Lord Lyon for an entire re-granting of the

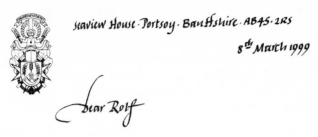

seaview House · Portsoy · Banffshire · AB45 · 2RS

8ᵗʰ March 1999

Dear Rolf

Figure 2: The headed writing paper of Ross Herald of Arms, including his coat of arms.

arms in your own name. It is worth noting that, unlike in England, Lord Lyon's Court has the power to imprison miscreants for misuse of arms.

Once a coat of arms has been granted it may be used in full or in part. Thus, either the full achievement or simply the crest might be used on stationery. Positioning of arms on stationery is dealt with in the section on headed writing paper below.

For more information on the use of, or indeed the granting of arms, in England and Wales you should contact The College of Arms, Queen Victoria Street, London EC4V 4BT (Telephone 020 7248 2762: Fax 020 7248 6448). In Scotland, contact The Court of The Lord Lyon, HM New Register House, Edinburgh EH1 3YT (Telephone 0131 556 7255: Fax 0131-557 2148).

Writing paper

There are several things to consider when it comes to the choice of writing paper, primarily: quality and weight; size; colour; the use of printed letterheads. The latter will be dealt with in a separate section below. In common with all

11

writing paper though, it should be plain and never lined, and of the best quality you can afford. Lined paper suggests that you cannot write in a straight line without help and can be reminiscent of school days. If you have trouble writing in a straight line, it is far better to use a pre-lined template which can be slipped under the paper whilst you are writing. You can even customise a template for your own purposes if, for example, you do not use headed paper and always put your address block in precisely the same place.

The best quality paper is hand made with a high 'rag content' and is watermarked. Rag content refers to the amount of cotton used in the paper and a watermark is the impression of the manufacturer's name or logo which can be seen if held up to the light. The higher the rag content, the better the paper will take both die stamping and writing with a fountain pen. Writing paper can be purchased in various weights and the trend currently is moving back towards heavier paper, that is, over 100 gm^2. Writing paper of 85 gm^2 or less is considered thin and above 160 gm^2 is not commonly available. Try to use paper which is thick enough so that, if you decide to write on both sides, you can do so without the ink showing through; you can achieve this with 140 gm^2.

Leaving weight aside, there are generally two types of paper available: woven or laid. Woven paper is of a smoother surface which, when held up to the light, has very close and even fibres. Laid paper has definite lines and ridges on the surface. Choose the type of paper carefully to best suit your style of handwriting. For example, if you write with a fountain pen with an italic nib, laid paper is difficult to use because of its ridged texture; the nib does not agree with it and tends to get caught on the little ridges. If the nib breaks a fibre in the surface of the paper, it can also cause the ink to bleed, thereby smudging the handwriting. Per-

12

fectly smooth, woven paper allows more options when it comes to the use of nib. So, in choosing your paper, find one which agrees with your other tools and the mechanics of your handwriting style. If you choose well, you will undoubtedly find that you use the same paper from the same supplier for many years. This also has the added advantage of developing a style or trademark in your stationery which will be immediately recognisable to your readers as they open your letters at the breakfast table.

Paper size depends primarily on the size of both your handwriting and the volume of text. That said, the large paper, such as A4, should normally only be used for business correspondence, where it is important to have the space both for the address block and salutation, etc. Social correspondence should normally be written on smaller paper. There are two traditional Imperial paper sizes, known as Kings or Duke. Kings is 8"×6¼" and Duke is 7"×5½" although the larger 9"×7" (as yet unnamed) is becoming more and more popular. These Imperial paper sizes give more choice between the two metric options of A4 or A5 where there is no in-between size. Whilst A5 is perfectly acceptable as writing paper, Imperial sizes give a more distinguished appearance.

There was a trend pre-1939 for fly-folded writing paper which gave us a nice alternative to the traditional Kings or Duke sizes. It measures 8½"×5¼" and opens like a greeting card, revealing four writing surfaces. Although it is now difficult to find on the shelves, it can be made to order. If you find some and decide to try it, I would recommend only writing on two surfaces, as though you are writing on both the front and inside back cover of a greeting card. Using only two of the surfaces and not the backs of either prevents any bleeding of ink. It is then folded once lengthways to fit into an envelope which measures 4¼"×5¼".

Remember to purchase enough envelopes to match your paper if you are buying an odd size or a colour which you might have difficulty finding again.

The colour of writing paper is again an opportunity to show personal style and taste. The most traditional colours are white, ivory or cream and various shades of blue. White and cream are also the most formal. Whilst using a more personalised colour is perfectly acceptable, avoid bright colours except for the most informal and frivolous of letters. Bright colours again smack of childish schoolboy crafts. Shades of blue, grey or even green are classical and stylish. Writing paper with a coloured edge is becoming very fashionable and allows you, along with the colour of the ink in the die stamp, to show personal flair. In choosing edged paper, avoid gold, silver and black. Black edged writing paper should be used exclusively to show mourning, when writing a letter of condolence or informing people of a death, for example. Black edged writing paper should always be plain and never die stamped.

Headed writing paper

Personalised stationery for social correspondence is by no means required, however it can look elegant and chic without being pretentious or exclusive. If you wish to have personal stationery printed, adhere as closely as possible to the general guidelines above as to choice of paper in colour, size and weight. How much information you wish to include in the heading is a personal choice but the currently acceptable trend is to include a full address with postal code and a telephone number. The old adage of 'less is more' is today seen as pretentious unless the house is very well known. An address described as 'Twee Cottage, Lower Slaughter, Gloucestershire' may well look rather pretentious, but if, on the other hand, you live in a castle in

Scotland, you might get away with deleting your postal code. Better to err on the side of practicality and include the proper postal address including a postcode. Your name is always omitted from a personal letterhead. Your address block may be either centred (including the telephone number), or right-justified. If you opt for the latter, traditionally the address goes on the right and a telephone number on the left. A right-justified address block is necessary if you wish to use an heraldic device to which you are entitled (see above) and this would normally be positioned in the top left corner. Unless using an heraldic device, the current trend is to use a centred address block as in the examples overleaf. Remember to order sufficient blank sheets of the same paper for continuation pages of letters longer than two sides; it is not normal to use more than one headed sheet per letter.

It is also important when considering headed paper to decide on an engraver's typeface which portrays the 'look' to which you aspire but is still easily readable. Printers will have examples of the different typefaces to choose from, additional examples of which are shown in figure 5. Choose carefully as you will undoubtedly live with your design for the duration of the time you live in your current house; a redesign may prove very costly.

Correspondence cards

Correspondence cards are normally printed on plain white, ivory or cream card but any muted colour is perfectly acceptable. Like all personal stationery, they should be of the best quality you can afford and should bear your name and address, including post code, a telephone number and even an email address may be included if desired. Die stamping or thermography is far more expensive and is not traditionally required for cards of this type where flat

15

22 BROOK STREET
LONDON W1X 7AK
0171-256 0874

6 PLACE SAINT GERMAIN
75001 PARIS
1 22 33. 44. 55.

13 ST. GEORGE STREET
LONDON WIR 9DE
0171-629 7301

123 Stanley Crescent
London W11 8PL
0171 - 629 8558

Via Bigli 9
Milano
02 - 48501112

40 Portland Place
London W1N 3DY
0171-629 8558

WARDENS LODGE
GLASTONBURY
SOMERSET TU12 6PW
01674 720695

90 EATON SQUARE
LONDON SW1W 9AS
0171-495 9230

Ovington Manor
Brackwater
Devon DV7 1GP
01364 828539

STRATHALLAN
BRIDGE OF EARN
PERTH PH13 9EL
01930 818181

720 PARK AVENUE
NEW YORK, NY 10021
(212) 123 4567

WILLIAM T. H. HAMILTON

ENGRAVED STYLES BY SMYTHSON ©

Figure 3: Sample address blocks in Smythson's own typefaces. It is most common for the address block to be centred at the top of a page of writing paper.

CALLIGRAPHY STYLES

Figure 4: Some of the more contemporary calligraphy styles which the Wren Press produce for their customers.

Elms House, Highworth, Wiltshire

HIBDEN HALL, PERTHSHIRE

10 The Boltons, SW7 3PW

FORESTERS LODGE, BIBURY, GLOUCESTERSHIRE

Wistaria Cottage, Upper Hemswick

Mowbray Court, Shropshire

GRANGE PARK, BROCKENHURST, HAMPSHIRE

40, Dolphin Square, London, SW7 3PL

The Old Rectory, Cirencester

2 UPPER CHEYNE ROW, SW3 5JN

GROSVENOR PLACE

Hepworth House, W1Y 5PZ

THE STUDIO, ST. IVES, CORNWALL

Tudor Cottage, Chester

The Parsonage, Moreton in Marsh

26 ELGIN CRESCENT, W8 6JE

RICHMOND MANOR, MARLBOROUGH

Cathedral Cloisters, Exeter, EX1 8NJ

Figure 5: The range of Smythson's engravers' typefaces. All reputable stationers will have similar examples of their typefaces from which you can choose.

printing is the norm. It is further traditional to have a line printed across the card below the name and address. Whilst there is certainly scope to personalise a correspondence card, sticking fairly closely to tradition is advisable.

Originally used only for notes to tradesmen, these cards may now be used for any informal correspondence in the same way that a postcard might be used. Informal invitations, brief notes of explanation to enclose with a cheque, for example, and notes of thanks are all occasions where a correspondence card may now be quite appropriately used. They may either be posted as a postcard, addressed and franked on the obverse, or enclosed in an envelope for more privacy.

Correspondence cards are normally half the size of personal writing paper and, if purchased from the same stationer, can be printed in the same typeface and in the same colour combination as your personal writing paper.

An alternative to a printed correspondence card is the picture postcard which may be purchased from galleries and museums. 'Art' cards are particularly suitable for this purpose.

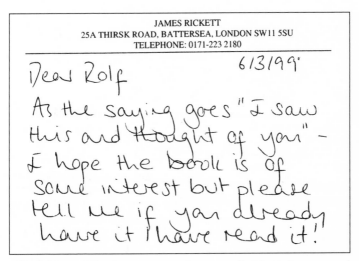

Figure 6: A friend's correspondence card. Note the centred address block, complete with the traditional underline.

Figure 7: Use your imagination with correspondence cards. The Wren Press produced this one on a heavy white 4½"×7" card bordered in blue with a calligraphy typeface.

Greeting cards

Before launching into a section on greeting cards, I should assert that they should be used most sparingly. Most occasions are better marked with a short letter. There are, however, cases where a greeting card is the most appropriate medium, often simply because of their traditional employment.

20

Occasions for sending greeting cards vary from the most traditional like Christmas, birthdays, and 'get well' cards to the less common retirements, good luck, passing exams, Christening, announcing a birth, etc. The list of cards is as endless as is the list of occasions which might come to mind and the proliferation of such cards is a mark of our commercial society. Apart from the differing occasion, there are two simple types of card, one where the manufacturer has done all the work for you and printed the greeting in an often poetic fashion and the other where the inside of the card is merely left blank. The choice of which of these two types to send is naturally that of the sender; however, I would strongly advise the use of the blank card if at all possible. Just think how disappointing it is to open a card from a loved one and find nothing but a signature below a pre-printed greeting. This can smack of insincerity, the one thing we obviously are not if we have gone to the trouble to send a card at all. Yet, in certain circumstances, perhaps in a difficult situation like a bereavement, the use of a pre-printed card might find the words which escape us. If at all possible, however, I would recommend a card with as little printed inside as possible. This allows us to put our literary skills to good use and pen a meaningful message which will, in the case of many people who keep cards, be treasured by the recipient for many years to come.

Change of address cards

Today, many choose not to advertise a change of address with a traditional card. Some prefer to email or telephone their friends and family with a new address. Whilst there may be less expensive and expedient ways of making such an announcement, they have serious drawbacks. Emails are often sent to business addresses and are thus often left in the office never to be transferred to a home address book.

21

CHANGE OF ADDRESS

———◆———

CHRISTOPHER & JENNIFER WREN

CHELSEA HOUSE
CHEYNE WALK
LONDON SW3 5DX

TELEPHONE: (020) 7352 7063

Paper	**Wren Wove Card**
Size	**4¼ x 6**
Typeface	**3**
Process	**Flatprinted**
Colour	**Black Ink**

Figure 8: A change of address card is normally flat printed on 4¼"×6" card.

A change of address is thus most correctly announced by the use of a printed card. It is normally 4¼"×6" and flat printed. It should include the new address and telephone number and may also include an effective date.

Envelopes

Envelopes for use with social correspondence are again a matter of personal choice. I prefer one which forces me to fold the letter only once and matches the paper. A letter folded twice smacks of an A4 letter in a long envelope, and white paper in a buff envelope somehow looks like you have run out of the proper ones. I stress again though, this is simply my personal choice. Traditionally however, envelopes for social correspondence should have deep diamond flaps and be of such a weight that the letter inside cannot be easily read. Tissue lining helps to overcome this problem but they are still more suitable for women than for men. Today, tissue lining is being used as much as a fashion statement as for security; they can even be produced so that the tissue matches the colour of the ink in the die stamp. Avoid envelopes with a printed disruptive pattern on the inside – they look rather cheap. Envelopes should be gummed and not self-sealing; they should be sealed when sent through the post but may be 'tucked-in' when hand delivered or when simply containing a card. Brown manila envelopes should never be used for social correspondence unless a letter needs to be double enveloped for privacy, for example, when you are forced to send a letter of a very personal nature to a business or military address where it may be opened by a secretary or other member of staff.

Business envelopes with a printed address show a degree of longevity and professionalism, both of which are unnecessary on private stationery. The use of sticky printed labels is tacky – avoid their use.

Addressing envelopes

In the English-speaking world, it is traditional to write the address on the front of the envelope so that it is approximately centred both horizontally and vertically. However, in France, for example, this is not the custom and the address is normally written centred between the top and bottom of the envelope but pushed to the far right leaving a large blank margin on the left. The return address should normally be written on the reverse of an envelope and not in the top left corner as is the practice on the other side of the Atlantic.

In some cases, personal assistants are given leave to open the post of their employer in order to present the letters with the required action already suggested in the top right-hand corner. In such a case, a personal letter might well be inadvertently opened by the PA. To avoid any potential embarrassment, it is permissible to include a privacy mark (ie. "PERSONAL") in either of the left-hand corners of the

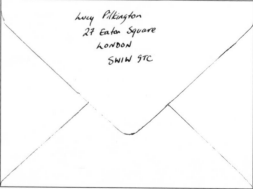

Figure 9: The obverse and reverse of an envelope. Although somewhat outdated, it is still traditional to capitalise the city name. Note the 'PERSONAL' privacy mark which alerts a secretary of the private nature of a letter.

envelope; this will alert a secretary to the private nature of the letter, which should then be delivered unopened to the desk of the addressee for his or her personal attention.

It is common to address a private letter to a gentleman at his club rather than at a home or business address.

Chapter 3

===

Forms of Address

Getting it right, when it comes to forms of address is very important, particularly if writing to a senior official when you are trying to make a good impression. Politicians, senior Civil Servants and diplomats, senior members of the clergy, Admirals, Generals, Air Marshals, to name but a few, will usually have what is known as an 'outer office'. This outer office will normally consist of a personal assistant, a secretary and/or an aide of some description. These personal staff are well used to telephone enquiries as to the correct form of address for their employer. You will normally get someone on the other end who is most helpful, so do not be embarrassed making such a call. Don't forget to ensure you make note of any 'postnominals' (letters after the name to denote honours, fellowships, academic degrees, and so on), a list of which is included below. A further detailed list of generic forms of address for most senior posts is included as an appendix to this book.

Precedence of letters

As the correct use of postnominals, or letters after a person's name, can be a very confusing subject, I shall attempt to simplify it as much as possible. The abbreviations 'Bt' or

'Bart' (for a baronet) or 'Esq', if applicable, precede all other letters. Other letters are then grouped, either by regulations or by custom, as follows:

1. Orders and decorations conferred by the Crown.
2. Appointments in the following order of precedence: Privy Councillor (PC), Aide de Camp to The Queen (ADC), Honorary Physician to The Queen (QHP), Honorary Surgeon to The Queen (QHS), Honorary Dental Surgeon to The Queen (QHDS), Honorary Nursing Sister to The Queen (QHNS), and Honorary Chaplain to The Queen (QHC).
3. Queen's Counsel (QC), Justice of the Peace (JP) and Deputy Lieutenant (DL).
4. University degrees.
5. (a) Religious orders.
   (b) Medical qualifications.
6. (a) Fellowships of learned societies.
   (b) Royal Academicians and Associations.
   (c) Fellowships, memberships, etc. of professional institutions, associations, etc.
   (d) Writers to the Signet.
7. Members of Parliament (MP).
8. Membership of one of the Armed Forces (RN, RM, regimental name or RAF).

It is important to keep the group together even if the order within the group presents difficulty.

So, for example, a military knight's correct form of address on an envelope might look thus, "Major General Sir John Trench, VC, KBE, CB, DSO, TD, ADC, DL, DPhil, FRS". The nature of the correspondence should determine which postnominals to use from groups 3, 4 and 5. For example, when writing to General Trench purely in his capacity as a soldier, DL, DPhil and FRS might be omitted.

A full list of postnominals is given below. I have excluded orders of chivalry and decorations which are no longer granted or common. Academic qualifications are representative of the most common degree qualifications taken from the Universities of Oxford, Cambridge, London and Birmingham. Not only does the position of the appropriate letters vary according to the granting university, but also to the name of the degree and the letters to indicate it. It should thus only be used as a rough guide.

VC	Victoria Cross	Precedes all letters including knights
GC	George Cross	After VC but before all other letters including knights
KG	Knight of the Garter	
KT	Knight of the Thistle	
GCB	Knight Grand Cross of the Order of the Bath	
OM	Order of Merit	Does not confer a knighthood
GCMG	Knight Grand Cross of the Order of St Michael & St George	
GCVO	Knight Grand Cross of the Royal Victorian Order	
GBE	Knight Grand Cross of the Order of the British Empire	
CH	Companion of Honour	Does not confer a knighthood
KCB	Knight Commander of the Order of the Bath	
KCMG	Knight Commander of the Order of St Michael & St George	

KCVO	Knight Commander of the Royal Victorian Order	
KBE	Knight Commander of the Order of the British Empire	
CB	Companion of the Order of the Bath	
CMG	Companion of the Order of St Michael & St George	
CVO	Commander of the Royal Victorian Order	
CBE	Commander of the Order of the British Empire	
DSO	Distinguished Service Order	
LVO	Lieutenant of the Royal Victorian Order	
OBE	Officer of the Order of the British Empire	
ISO	Imperial Service Order	
MVO	Member of the Royal Victorian Order	
MBE	Member of the Order of the British Empire	
KStJ, CStJ, OStJ, etc.	The Venerable Order of St John (various grades)	Not included as postnominals except on correspondence within the Order.
RRC	Royal Red Cross	
DSC	Distinguished Service Cross	
MC	Military Cross	
DFC	Distinguished Flying Cross	
ARRC	Associate of the Royal Red Cross	
AFC	Air Force Cross	
DCM	Distinguished Conduct Medal	
CGM	Conspicuous Gallantry Medal	

GM	George Medal	
DSM	Distinguished Service Medal	
MM	Military Medal	
DFM	Distinguished Flying Medal	
AFM	Air Force Medal	
SGM	Medal for Saving Life at Sea	
CPM	Colonial Police Medal for Gallantry	
QGM	Queen's Gallantry Medal	
BEM	British Empire Medal	Not part of the Order of the British Empire and is no longer awarded
QPM	Queen's Police Medal	
QFSM	Queen's Fire Service Medal	
ERD	Army Emergency Reserve Decoration	
TD	Territorial Decoration	
ED	Efficiency Decoration	
RD	Decoration for Officers of the Royal Naval Reserve	
AE	Air Efficiency Award	
CD	Canadian Forces Decoration	
DD	Doctor of Divinity	
LLD	Doctor of Laws	
MD	Doctor of Medicine	
DLit	Doctor of Letters	
DSocSc	Doctor of Social Science	
DLitt/LittD	Doctor of Literature	
DSc/ScD	Doctor of Science	
DMus/MusD	Doctor of Music	
PhD	Doctor of Philosophy	
MSocSc	Master of Social Sciences	
MCom	Master of Commerce	
MPharm	Master of Pharmacy	

MEd	Master of Education	
LLM	Master of Laws	
MusM	Master of Music	
MLitt	Master of Letters	
MPhil	Master of Philosophy	
MS	Master of Surgery	
MSc	Master of Science	
MA	Master of Arts	Never used in social correspondence
BSc	Bachelor of Science	
VetMB	Bachelor of Veterinary Medicine	
LLB	Bachelor of Laws	
BSocSc	Bachelor of Social Science	
BCom	Bachelor of Commerce	
BDS	Bachelor of Dental Surgery	
BD	Bachelor of Divinity	
BCL	Bachelor of Civil Law	
BM/MB	Bachelor of Medicine	
BS	Bachelor of Surgery	
BLitt	Bachelor of Literature	
BMus/MusB	Bachelor of Music	
BPhil	Bachelor of Philosophy	
BA	Bachelor of Arts	Never used in social correspondence
BEd/EdB	Bachelor of Education	

The use of 'Esq.' and 'Master'

Esquire is technically the social rank above a gentleman. One was traditionally not seen to have become an esquire until attaining the rank of captain in the army (or its equivalent in the other forces or in civilian life). A subaltern, as a gentleman, was thus always referred to as 'Mr'. In modern days, all men are given the courtesy title of 'Esq.' in social and business correspondence, although this is technically incorrect.

At Eton and some other public schools, it is traditional to be styled as an esquire immediately upon entering the school. The style of 'Master', at one time used for boys up to the age of twelve or thirteen has largely gone out of fashion. If used now, it should be restricted to boys under the age of eight. More sensibly they should simply be addressed by name.

The use of 'Ms'

Many women are addressed as 'Ms' in business corres-pondence as the equivalent of 'Mr.' Whilst this is accept-able, many women do not like this style and it is wise to attempt to find out before writing. It is most unusual to style a woman as 'Ms' in social correspondence, where she should be referred to either as 'Miss' or 'Mrs', unless she has a particular desire to be styled as 'Ms'. If a woman continues to use her maiden name after marriage for con-venience in business, she should continue to be referred to as 'Miss' unless she makes it clear that she prefers otherwise.

Chapter 4

===

Pens and Ink

A good quality fountain pen is always the weapon of choice when letter writing socially. Today, there are many implements to choose from and the nearest biro tends to be what we immediately reach for. Yet, biros tend not to give a very good account of a person's handwriting and make a rather rough and uneven line of ink. Similarly, they often smudge in a rather unattractive way. If your handwriting is not the very best, a biro will not help you to improve and in fact may alter it beyond recognition. I was asked recently, after filling out an application form, if I had had someone else fill out the manuscript sections for me. The majority of the form I had childishly printed in black ball-point pen whilst the longhand questions I completed in my 'normal hand', using my fountain pen. It had not occurred to me at the time of completion, but I quite agreed with the interviewer that it did indeed look as though two different people had worked on the application form. All that to say, your handwriting, like mine, may improve significantly with the use of a good quality ink pen if chosen carefully. It took me several weeks of shopping to find the right pen but I finally happened upon a lovely shop in Burlington Arcade off Piccadilly. Peter Woolf runs an amazing little shop which, despite its unobtrusive appearance, is one of the largest independent dealers of antique pens in the world. They also stock all the major makes of modern pens, but, he stresses, only those which may be serviced properly in the future. They also have their own pen restorers, based in London, which were dubbed by *Country Life* as a 'National Treasure'.[1]

When a customer first walks into Penfriend, Peter is already studying the customer's hands. He needs to know the size of the hand and whether the person is left or right-handed. From there he asks them to begin writing so that he can see the speed at which they write as well as the kind of pressure they exert on the paper. Only when the style of handwriting has been determined, can he start to advise a customer on the choice of nib. Unlike a biro, a fountain pen has a tip which allows the ink to run on to the paper in a controlled flow. The nib also determines the shape of the line left on the paper. Penfriend stocks around 20 different nibs for some pens, one of which is likely to match the customer's hand – if not, the workshop can grind the nib to fit the writer.

If you are not able to make use of an expert eye at somewhere like Penfriend, these are the sort of considerations you should make before making your purchase:

- Grip – does the pen feel good? Is it too big or too small for your hand?
- Weight – a pen should feel substantial and apply its own force on the paper without having to press down too hard.
- Attractiveness – do you like the look of a pen which you may well use for the rest of your life?
- Price – is it within your means without scrimping on quality? Do you want to spend a great deal on a pen if you have a propensity to lose small objects?

---

[1] Country Life edition September 21, 1995

- Nib – does the nib suit, or indeed flatter, your style of handwriting? Is it necessary to have the nib ground to better suit? Considering an oblique nib can make poor handwriting more readable.
- Ink – most pens use ink cartridges these days, but if you wish to use bottled ink, consider getting a converter. If you use a filler, consider whether the filler is an easy-to-use mechanism? Can you use it properly or will you forever be making a mess? Can you use any type of ink or does the manufacturer recommend a particular one? If so, why?

Naturally, shopping around will give you a good idea of price and practical usability, and your requirements will evolve as you move from shop to shop. Remember that a pen that improves the look of your handwriting may justify spending that little bit of extra money.

There are of course many other implements which we might use for letter writing which do not fall into the category of a biro. There are many pens on the market which imitate a fountain pen and are far less expensive. They range from the 'roller ball' to calligraphy pens which mimic an italic fountain pen rather well. The only caution attached to the use of any of these pens is that they may use an ink which can bleed on certain types of paper. I would

OB   B   STUB   OM   M   F   XF

Figure 10: Some of the more commonly available pen nibs and an example of the line each draws. If need be, nibs can generally be ground to suit a particular style of handwriting.

recommend taking along a piece of your favourite station-ery when pen shopping so that you can test the pen on the sort of paper you will likely be using at home.

The final thing to mention in a section on writing imple-ments is that a pencil is never acceptable for correspon-dence, whether social or business. Writing in pencil, because of its temporary nature, should be reserved for shopping lists.

The signature

Earlier we mused over our adolescent days having been spent practising our signature, in an attempt to get it just right. For a whole day spent using a word processor, often all a reader sees of our own handwriting after all that effort is our signature. It is thus worth spending time getting it right. A sloppy illegible signature appended at the foot of a letter in biro says far less about the writer than does a strong and stylish moniker in bold black ink. If you have been using the same signature for many years it may be difficult to change it; yet, the pain and suffering of changing a signature may be well worth the hassle if it increases your credibility on paper. Consider using the opportunity of changing jobs or moving house to alter your signature – just remember to tell your bank so that they do not start returning your cheques.

The medium can be the message

A final word on tools before we move into the different types of correspondence we might encounter. I mentioned both in the introduction and again at the beginning of the section on stationery that the medium can in some in-stances become the message. That is to say that your message may well be lost if the way you decide to deliver it is inappropriate. Business letters should naturally be typed, to show a degree of professionalism and clarity. A letter to a lover, on the other hand, could seem cold and distant unless written in your own hand. Worse yet, sending a love letter by fax would certainly give a poor impression not to mention its lack of privacy.

All that to say, be very careful in the way you decide to convey you message:

- think carefully about the physical medium (paper, ink, colours, etc);
- decide on an appropriate mode of delivery (by hand, post, fax, etc);
- be sympathetic to your audience, that is, write in a way which will be plainly understood;
- consider timing, especially if you are asking a favour or breaking difficult news (choose a time when your recipient will be most responsive to your message).

Chapter 5

===

Topping and Tailing

We have now looked in depth at the tools of letter writing, but before we delve into the mechanics, perhaps there are a few other points to make about getting started.

Letter headings

Much confusion can be avoided by inserting the correct style by which the sender of a letter wishes to be addressed on all outgoing post. This may be done with the use of headed stationery but can also simply be written in by hand. It is common in the Armed Forces to top a hand-written letter with the words, "From: Captain Jonathan Forrester CBE Royal Navy" for example. This gives the reader the correct style with which the writer should be addressed, including postnominals, for any return correspondence. This information may well be readily available, but it will save your reader time in penning their response. However, the use of 'Mr' or 'Esq.' should always be omitted as this can look rather pompous. Placing your name at the top of the address block has the added advantage over printing your name under the signature as it is not customary to include postnominals here.

Beginning and ending a letter

There are myriad ways you might begin and end a letter. The level of formality is the deciding factor, and you can achieve much in the tone of a letter by using a suitable beginning and end. Needless to say, if your salutation and subscription are very formal, the language of the text needs to be suitably formal as well; in the same way, you would never start a letter to "Dear John", "I have the honour to inform you of . . ."

To help you get this right, I have included a full list of the most commonly used salutations and subscriptions. Please see the table beginning on page 94 in the section entitled, '*Conducting business from home.*'

Chapter 6

===

Invitations and Replies

Royal Commands

Invitations from the Sovereign are, by custom, considered to be commands. Invitations from Her Majesty will normally be sent by:

- The Lord Steward of the Household for a State Banquet;
- The Lord Chamberlain for all other major court functions such as a Garden Party, Wedding, Funeral or Memorial Service; or,
- The Master of the Household to all domestic functions given by Her Majesty at Buckingham Palace or another royal residence.

As commands, invitations from the Sovereign should be treated as such when replying. The reply should be worded with this in mind and addressed to the member of the Household who issued the invitation.

Garden Parties are slightly different in that an acknowledgement is not required unless a guest is unable to attend. An admission card will accompany the invitation which must be surrendered for entry into the grounds of the Palace. If a guest is unable to attend, this card must be returned.

The Lord Chamberlain is
commanded by Her Majesty to invite

Lieutenant Rolf Kurth, R.N.

to a Garden Party
at the Palace of Holyroodhouse
on Thursday 6th July 1995 from 4 to 6 pm

Figure 11: An invitation to a Royal Garden Party at the Palace of Holyroodhouse held in Edinburgh each July. An invitation to Buckingham Palace would look very similar. These invitations are commonly known as 'stiffies' because of the weight of the card on which they are printed.

An invitation from the Sovereign might be worded something like:

> The Master of the Household
> is Commanded by Her Majesty to invite
> Sir Walter and Lady Seymour
> to Luncheon at Balmoral
> on Wednesday, 25 August at 1 o'clock.

Suitable wording for the acceptance of such an invitation might be:

41

> Sir Walter and Lady Seymour present their compliments to the Master of the Household, and have the honour to obey Her Majesty's Command to luncheon on 25 August at 1 o'clock.

If you are unable to attend, and there must be a very good reason for such non-acceptance (such as an illness, prior business engagement which would severely let others down or a significant family event such as a wedding), you might word your reply thus:

> Sir Walter and Lady Seymour present their compliments to the Master of the Household, and much regret that they will be unable to obey Her Majesty's Command to Luncheon on 25 August owing to the illness of Lady Seymour.

Remember a reply declining a Royal Command, unlike other social invitations, should always include the reason for not accepting.

If it is appropriate to pen a thankyou letter, such as after a State Banquet or luncheon, but never after a Garden Party, it should be addressed to the member of the Household who issued the invitation. You should ask him to convey your thanks to Her Majesty for... etc. Never get too personal and keep such a letter very short and to the point. This is not the place to comment on the new wallpaper.

Invitations by Her Majesty Queen Elizabeth The Queen Mother

Invitations issued by the Comptroller of the Household of Her Majesty Queen Elizabeth The Queen Mother should be treated as Royal Commands, in the same way as for the Sovereign. The Queen Mother is the only other member of the Royal Family who is accorded the courtesy of this tradition. Replies should thus be worded as above.

Invitations by other Members of the Royal Family

Invitations by other members of the Royal Family should not be treated as commands. They will normally be issued by a member of their own Household, to whom the reply should be addressed. In all other ways, the same form should be used as for the Sovereign.

Invitations to formal events

It is impossible to go into great detail on every formal invitation which might be issued, and as such I will only

The Purse Bearer is commanded by

Her Royal Highness The Princess Royal

Lord High Commissioner

to the General Assembly of the Church of Scotland

to invite

Lieutenant Rolf Kurth

to an Afternoon Party in the Garden of The Palace of Holyroodhouse
on Saturday 18th May 1996 from 3.30 to 5.30 p.m.

Dress informal
No reply required   THIS IS NOT A CARD OF ADMITTANCE

Figure 12: An invitation sent in the name of the Princess Royal. Unlike a strictly private invitation by a member of the Royal Family, this invitation was sent as a command because of HRH's capacity as Lord High Commissioner.

paint with a very broad brush. There are many occasions when a simple social invitation will not do and you are thus forced to come up with a printed card which may be sent out to those you hope will attend your event. To illustrate, I have included examples of many of the invitations to events which I have attended or been party to organising. By looking at these, you will note that there are many different ways to word the card, but they all contain the same basic information. Some are from individuals (or in the name of individuals), others are from organisations or established bodies. If you have been tasked to issue such an invitation, you might choose one from those on the following pages which most closely matches your needs; the example can then be adapted in style and content for your own event.

WMP

THE MODERATOR REQUESTS THE PRESENCE OF

Lt R. Kurtk R.N.

at a Dinner to be held within the Palace of Holyroodhouse,

by gracious permission of Her Majesty the Queen, on

Saturday 27th May 1995 at 7.00p for 7.30p

EVENING, HIGHLAND OR MESS DRESS DECORATIONS

This invitation must be presented at the entrance

Figure 13: A formal invitation to a dinner which doubled as a ticket for entry.

Figure 14: An 'RPC' from the Lieutenant Governor of the Isle of Man. 'RSVP' should more correctly be in the bottom left hand corner and 'dress' in the right.

Figure 15: A formal invitation to dinner worded so that it could be kept for a scrapbook. As in the example above, 'Pour memoir' should ideally be in the bottom left corner.

45

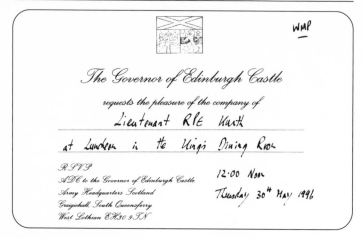

Figure 16: Another more formal invitation. As you can see, with enough spaces left blank, these can be used for any occasion.

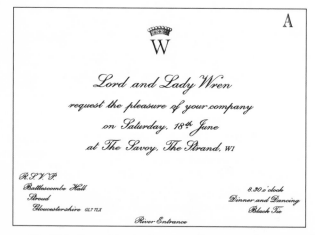

Figure 17: This formal invitation was die stamped onto card of such a weight it could be considered a 'stiffy'. Its edges are bevelled and both the monogram and coronet are gilded.

Social invitations

There are many and varied social events which require us to extend an invitation to our home or other venue. From casual coffee with the ladies in the late morning, to lunch, afternoon tea in the garden, to formal dinner parties or even an evening cocktail party. The list of possible events is endless but the general form of an invitation is fairly standard and can be issued in one of three ways. One may simply write a letter or short note, even using a correspondence card, as mentioned earlier. If more formality is required, you can use either a printed invitation card or use a pre-printed 'at home' card. The former is the most formal and would normally be used only for the grandest occasions like an important birthday, a wedding anniversary or a charity event which is being held in the garden. The latter is the less formal of the two but maintains a certain dignity and gives the recipient the impression that this is an event of some note. Whatever way you choose to invite someone to a social occasion, writing it down in some way is by far preferable to a simple telephone conversation. By all means follow up an invitation by telephone to remind a friend of dinner, for example, but by first putting the invitation in writing you avoid any potential confusion. By using an invitation card or a letter you are explicitly informing the guest of the following important pieces of information:

- Names of the host and/or hostess – to whom your guest will invariably write the thankyou letter.
- Nature of the event – dinner, kitchen supper, cocktail party... this will have an effect on the way your guests prepare for the engagement. Should they bring the obligatory bottle of wine for a dinner party? Would taking a partner be appropriate?
- Date – include the day of the week to avoid any confusion.

47

- Time – '8 for 8.30pm' implies that you intend to be sitting down by 8.30pm.
- Location – include the address if your guests are unfamiliar with the venue and perhaps even include a map in the envelope if it is difficult to get to.
- Dress – black tie, lounge suit, casual… all have an explicit meaning. Consult *Debrett's New Guide to Etiquette and Modern Manners* for additional information on this subject. The key here is to save your guests any embarrassment in arriving significantly over or under dressed.
- RSVP or pour memoir – dealt with in more detail below, but put simply, do you need your guests to reply to the invitation or are you already sure who will attend?

To miss any of the above information is to set both yourself and your guest up for a possible embarrassing situation. Social engagements are meant to be enjoyable and the traditions or, if you like, rules, which we have surrounding these occasions are there to help us. These social rules are not to make entertaining difficult but to free both hosts and guests to enjoy themselves without any danger of a social *faux pas*.

'at Home' cards

The 'at Home' card and the phrase 'at Home' share their origins, predominantly in the 17th century, when a lady would, as the phrase explicitly suggests, be at home to a caller. She would inform her butler that she was either 'at Home' or not, as fit her mood, should any callers arrive. The 'at Home' card became commonplace to send to friends so that they would know when to call on a lady, thus saving any embarrassment of being sent away. It was almost a general invitation to an open house, if you will.

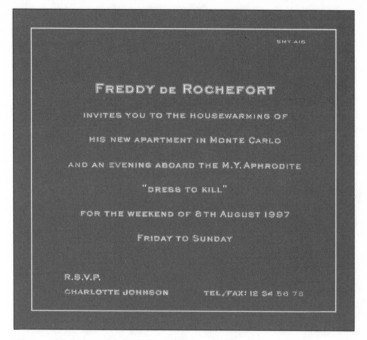

Figure 18: Even a fun invitation has all the information you need both to reply and to attend.

'At Home' cards should always be issued in the name of the hostess and never jointly. Gentlemen should never use 'at Home' cards but must always issue invitations in the form of "requesting the pleasure of the company of..." Whilst not technically correct, you should not be 'at Home' other than at home; however this rule has been relaxed of late. It is now quite common for people to be "at Home at the Dorchester Hotel for a lunch", for example.

Nowadays, 'at Home' cards have come to be a common blank invitation card which one may use for any occasion,

Charlie

SMY AI

Mrs John de Vere

at Home

for lunch
on Sunday, 29th August
at 1 o'clock

Pour memoir

~~R.S.V.P~~
2 Collingham Mews,
London SW7 2HQ.

Casual

Figure 19: 'At Home' cards, printed blank, allow you to insert as much or as little information as you like. RSVP can be struck out and replaced with 'pour memoir' if the guest has already accepted by telephone and you are sure they are planning to attend.

often inserting after the printed 'at Home' the words 'for lunch' or any other such description of the event. Whilst their use is acceptable for any occasion, they are still most correctly used for social invitations during the day. An 'at Home' card would not be technically correct for an invitation to dinner or a cocktail party. In its place, a similarly available pre-printed invitation with wording such as the "request the pleasure of your company" example below would more correctly be used. If you wish to personalise these, you might have cards printed, adding your name and perhaps even an armorial device (if you are so entitled).

50

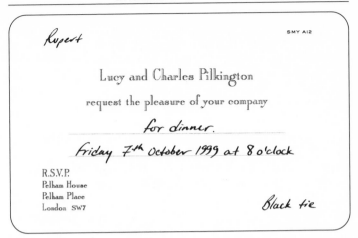

Rupert

SMY A12

Lucy and Charles Pilkington

request the pleasure of your company

for dinner.

Friday 7th October 1999 at 8 o'clock

R.S.V.P.
Pelham House
Pelham Place
London SW7

Black tie

Figure 20: An invitation requesting the pleasure of your company, as sent out by a couple. 'At Home' cards are never sent out jointly.

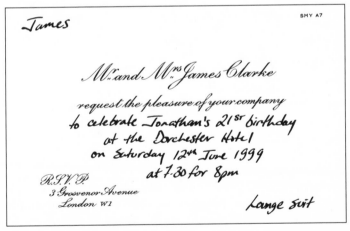

James

SMY A7

Mr and Mrs James Clarke

request the pleasure of your company

to celebrate Jonathan's 21st birthday
at the Dorchester Hotel
on Saturday 12th June 1999
at 7.30 for 8pm

R.S.V.P
3 Grosvenor Avenue
London W1

Large suit

Figure 21: If 'Mr & Mrs' are used, then only the husband's name should be included. Dress should always be included to avoid any embarrassment.

RSVP and 'pour memoir'

RSVP or *repondéz s'il vous plait* simply translates as 'please reply' and exhorts the invitee to make their intention of attending or not plain to the host. A reply should be made as soon as practicable to allow the host to plan for numbers. The other notation often seen on invitation cards is *'pour memoir'* . This notation is normally used when the card is sent only as a reminder of the invitation and your attendance has already been confirmed either in person or by telephone. If you have your own cards printed, it is advisable to have them produced as RSVP cards. It is perfectly acceptable to cross out the RSVP and insert *'pour memoir'* in manuscript. Cards with both notations printed so that one

Charler Pilkington thanks
Freddy de Rochefort for his kind
Invitation to the housewarming
of his new apartment in
Monte Carlo and an evening
on board the MY Aphrodite
for the weekend of 8 August 1997
and has much pleasure in
accepting.

15 June 1997

Figure 22: A written reply to accept an invitation. The same basic format is used for any event.

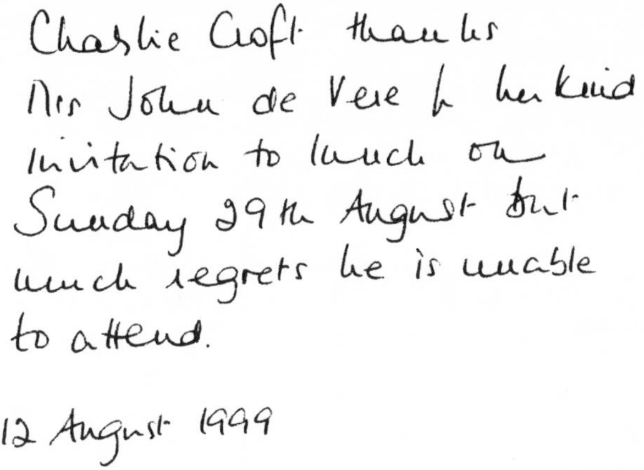

Charlie Croft thanks
Mrs John de Vere for her kind
Invitation to lunch on
Sunday 29th August but
much regrets he is unable
to attend.

12 August 1999

Figure 23: A written reply declining an invitation. Note that the reason for declining is never included (except for royal invitations as discussed earlier); a separate letter should always be written.

can later be crossed out are less desirable and should be avoided.

RSVP or *pour memoir* is always printed in the bottom left corner of the card. Other information, such as the dress, timings, etc. should be placed in the bottom right corner.

Once you have replied to an invitation, it is always wise to make note of your response on the card itself. I was taught to use the initials *WMP* (indicating that I had replied that I would attend 'With Much Pleasure') or conversely, *MRU* (that I Much Regretted that I was Unable to attend). A simple 'A' or 'D' for accept or decline may be more your style but choose one form of notation which you will remember and stick with it. The occasion should then be entered into your diary before being placed on your mantel with the myriad other invitations.

Letters to invite

The other way of inviting someone to a social occasion is to write a letter of invitation. There is no real set format for such a letter, but in doing so, you should be careful to include all the important information mentioned in the introduction to this section. The tone of the letter may be more or less formal, depending on the nature of the occasion and can even include such things as a guest list. This is sometimes a reassuring point to make, particularly if someone is unlikely to know any of the other guests, or for a formal gathering where to not have heard of someone may be insulting. It also gives your guests the opportunity to discreetly request that you "not put me next to that bore, Jonathan, whom I sat next to at the Jones's last week". Whilst such a request might at face value seem somewhat rude, it could save an otherwise disastrous dinner party.

Telephone to remind?

As mentioned earlier, there is nothing wrong with a quick telephone call to remind your guests of an event, particularly if the invitation was sent out with a long lead time. Of course, you may wish to veil this as a social call ending simply with "Looking forward to seeing you on Friday night". This reminds your guest to consult their diary without being put on the spot and potentially embarrassed.

Chapter 7

===

Marking the Occasions of Life

There are many occasions in life where a greeting card may be the first medium we reach for to express our thoughts or best wishes. I would argue that whilst a greeting card may well be suitable, a letter penned in your own hand is received with more pleasure.

Births

In addition to telephone calls to close relatives and prospective godparents, and an announcement in the newspaper, births are normally announced by sending out a card. These can be purchased pre-printed from a stationer on which simply the names of parents and new-born, dates, weight, etc. need to be entered in manuscript. Alternatively, a card can be die stamped or flat printed which includes all of the above information. Some have been known to have the die silver plated which, when kept for use as a paperweight, can be a lovely memento of a child's birth.

The card is normally in the region of $2\frac{1}{2}"\times4"$ and folded. Unlike more formal stationery, it can be decorative and coloured in keeping with the gender of the child. The text of such a card should read something like:

Lucy and Charles Pilkington
are pleased to announce the birth of their son,
James Graham Alexander,
on 27th August, 1999 at 5.17am.
He weighed 7 pounds, 8 ounces.

Some proud parents even include a small photograph of the new-born, although I would recommend resisting this urge.

If you receive a card announcing a birth, it is polite to pen a quick note of congratulations, either on writing paper or a correspondence card. Be conscious that a ringing telephone or an unexpected knock at the door might be the last thing the parents will want to hear as they come to terms with the new arrival to their home.

Christening

As a Christening is normally a very small affair, it is unusual and not expected to issue invitations. Likewise, for the small party which is traditionally held afterwards for the close family, godparents and clergy, no formal invitations need be sent. A newspaper announcement of the birth is also common practice.

Announcing an engagement

An engagement is most often announced in the newspaper, except to close family and friends where a telephone call or a personal visit is the more common practice. Public announcements vary from publication to publication, and I suggest you consult *Debrett's New Guide to Etiquette and Modern Manners* to get a better feel for the whole subject. Some couples use an event, such as an engagement party, to announce the happy news; if this is a road you wish to go down, the following is a very good example of the wording of an invitation:

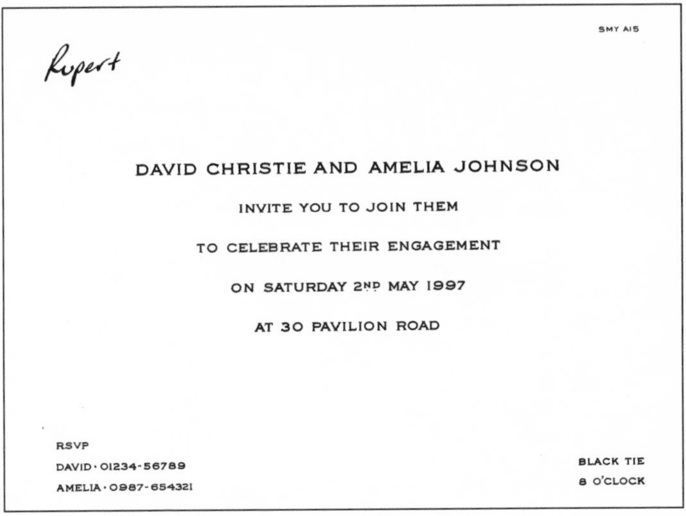

SMY A15

Rupert

DAVID CHRISTIE AND AMELIA JOHNSON

INVITE YOU TO JOIN THEM

TO CELEBRATE THEIR ENGAGEMENT

ON SATURDAY 2ND MAY 1997

AT 30 PAVILION ROAD

RSVP
DAVID · 01234-56789
AMELIA · 0987-654321

BLACK TIE
8 O'CLOCK

Figure 24: An engagement party invitation.

It is customary to write to the newly engaged to congratulate, but never to the couple jointly, even if they live together. The man's friends should write to him and the woman's to her. It is customary to never actually use the word 'congratulate' in a letter to the bride – it is seen to suggest entrapment. This is not so in letters to the groom.

Birthday parties

Birthday parties should always be announced by an invitation card "requesting the pleasure of the company of..." or "invites you to join her for...". They should never be sent as 'at Home' cards.

The two examples below illustrate the ideal way to send out a birthday invitation.

David and Amelia

SMY-AIO

Rupert Alexander

requests the pleasure of your company

to celebrate his 30th Birthday

at Spencer House

R.S.V.P.
112 Brook Street
London WIX 7AK

Black Tie
8 o'clock

Figure 25: An invitation to a birthday party sent by a gentleman. Note that a gentleman is never 'at Home'.

Freddy

SMY AI3

VICTORIA CHRISTIE

INVITES YOU TO JOIN HER

FOR HER 40TH BIRTHDAY

ON SATURDAY 12TH MAY

AT THE IVY

R.S.V.P.
01233 - 480136

8 O'CLOCK

Figure 26: Another birthday party invitation. If a venue or house is well known, you may omit the address without fear of confusion.

Wedding invitations

In the United Kingdom, unlike the United States and other parts of the western world, wedding invitations traditionally follow a set form. These long-standing conventions need not be seen as stuffy, but may actually grant the bride and groom or their parents a certain amount of immunity from criticism were they to attempt a more trendy approach. I would thus always recommend using the format of the traditional, formal invitation. If you decide to deviate from this structure to add an air of informality to the occasion, the same basic information must always be included, namely: who is to be married; the names of the hosts and their relationship to the former; locations of the ceremony and/or reception; date; time; and finally, where the reply should be sent.

The cost of printing will no doubt add significantly to the wedding budget, but if possible a wedding invitation should be die stamped in black ink from an engraved copperplate on heavy white or cream card. The typeface most traditionally used is copperplate. Flat printing should always be avoided but thermography or other raised printing may be used to cut cost. Cards should normally measure between 7"×5½" to 8"×6" (the latter being the most classic); larger than this is vulgar, as are gilded edges or other excesses. Unlike most invitation cards, wedding invitations retain the tradition of an upright folded sheet, somewhat like a greeting card, with the inside left blank.

It is acceptable to insert a blank line after "requests the pleasure of the company of" as on an 'at Home' card; however this is unnecessary and outdated. Simply have "requests the pleasure of your company..." printed and write the guests' names on the top left corner of the card. Wedding invitations should normally be sent out at least

59

eight weeks prior to the happy day. If it is to be a summer wedding, it is advisable to increase this lead time to allow guests to plan holidays around the wedding day.

The traditional wedding invitation

Today, many like to add a trendy slant to their stationery, but most still like all aspects of the wedding to be very traditional, from the dress to the cake to the stationery. An

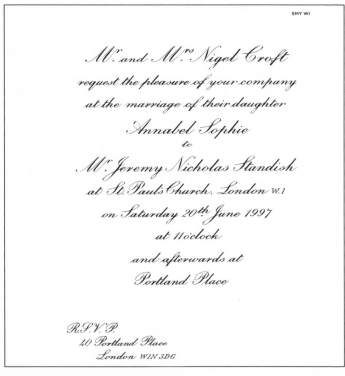

Figure 27: A formal wedding invitation with the traditional wording.

60

example of such a traditional invitation can be found below where both parents of the bride are the host and hostess. It has been produced on folded 8"×6" stiff, white card, and die stamped in black ink. Further advice on the wording of wedding invitations can be found in *Debrett's Correct Form* if there is a less than traditional family situation (e.g. the bride's parents are divorced and have remarried but still wish to host the wedding jointly).

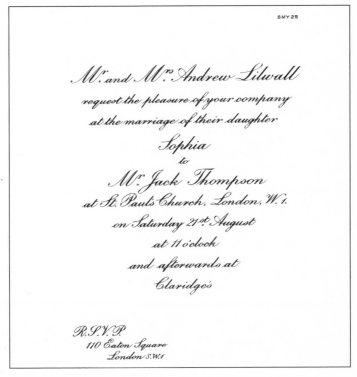

Figure 28: Another example of a formal wedding invitation on 6"×8" folded card.

Example of informal wedding invitations

The example below might be particularly appropriate when the couple is older, have been married before, or where the involvement of the parents does not extend to hosting the wedding.

It is with joy that we,
Mary-Anne Manson
and
Ronald Richard Smith
invite you to share
in a celebration of love
as we exchange our marriage vows
on Saturday, the fifteenth of August
nineteen hundred and ninety-nine
at six forty-five in the evening
Christ Church
Old McLellan Road
Langley, British Columbia

Replying to wedding invitations

As with the invitation itself, a reply to a wedding invitation traditionally follows a set form, and should be used without significant deviation. The reply should be handwritten with a fountain pen on good quality writing paper and in the third person. If the invitation was sent to you "and guest", the reply should include the guest's name. If, at a later date you are forced to change your guest, it should only be done with the host's express permission.

If an invitation has to be refused, the reason should not be mentioned in the text of the formal reply. In such a case, another informal note should be included with the formal

Mr. and Mrs. Christopher Wren

request the pleasure of the company of

at the marriage of their daughter

Jennifer to Mr. Robin Bird

at the Church of St. Francis, Chelsea, SW3

on Saturday, 1st May at 3 o'clock

and afterwards at 14 Birdcage Walk, SW1

R.S.V.P. 15 Lots Road, London SW10 0QJ

VIII

Figure 29: A less traditional invitation, illustrated on a 6"×7¼" folded card. Note that whilst adding an air of informality, such invitations should retain the same basic information.

reply, thanking the hosts for the invitation, apologising and briefly detailing the reason for the refusal. Examples of standard replies are set out below.

Notice that in common with any formal reply, the letter should be written by hand on plain writing paper, omitting both the name of the sender and the date, which will be obvious from the text.

Reply cards

Reply cards are becoming more common on this side of the Atlantic, although they do not traditionally form part of a

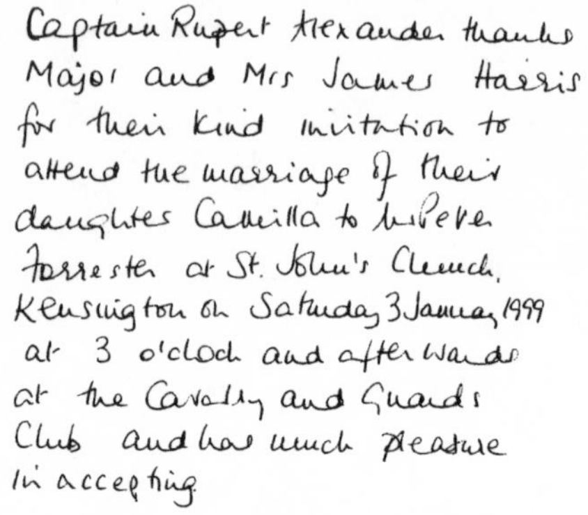

Captain Rupert Alexander thanks Major and Mrs James Harris for their kind invitation to attend the marriage of their daughter Camilla to Mr Peter Forrester at St. John's Church, Kensington on Saturday 3 January 1999 at 3 o'clock and afterwards at the Cavalry and Guards Club and has much pleasure in accepting

Figure 30: Acceptance of a wedding invitation.

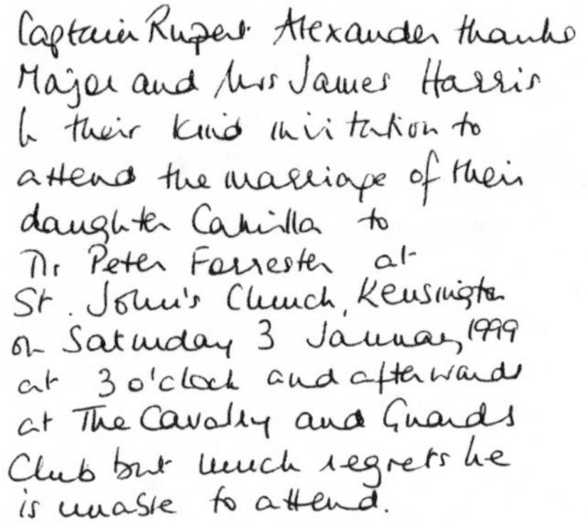

Captain Rupert Alexander thanks Major and Mrs James Harris for their kind invitation to attend the marriage of their daughter Camilla to Mr Peter Forrester at St. John's Church, Kensington on Saturday 3 January 1999 at 3 o'clock and afterwards at The Cavalry and Guards Club but much regrets he is unable to attend.

Figure 31: Declining a wedding invitation.

couple's wedding stationery. They are however, very useful when organising a large event, such as a wedding, when going through hundreds of handwritten replies may prove an ominous task. Reply cards are normally of small correspondence card size and are always flat printed. They

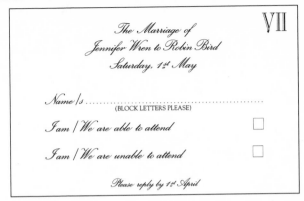

Figure 32: Example of a reply card. In this case the return address was printed on the reverse so that it could be returned as a postcard.

are normally worded such that a guest simply needs to fill in their name(s) and delete where not applicable to indicate attendance or non-attendance. If you have been offered a place for a guest, this is the place to inform your host of the person's name.

A reply card negates the need to write a reply but, like a letter, should be returned as soon as possible to allow the couple to make their plans. If you are unable to attend, always write a separate letter apologising and informing of the reason; never try to explain on the reply card itself.

Thankyou cards

An 'informal' is the correct term for a small folded thankyou card which is usually die stamped on the front with the first names of both the bride and groom. They are used to thank their guests for gifts or for some other small favour or bit of assistance a wedding guest might have given. These

65

Figure 33: An informal will normally have only the first names of the couple. It should be folded and opens from the bottom to reveal the writing surface.

are not used to thank ushers, groomsmen or bridesmaids for their services, which should be done using normal writing paper. An informal may, however, be sent to one of the wedding party in addition to a thankyou letter, but only to thank them specifically for a gift.

Death and letters of condolence

The announcement of a death is, not dissimilarly to birth, done in person or on the telephone to close family and friends. A newspaper announcement is always appropriate however, and is the way the majority of acquaintances and colleagues will learn of the sad news.

Once a death has been announced, it is normal to send a letter of condolence to the spouse or partner of the deceased as soon as you hear. It should not be overly sentimental and is not directed specifically at how the loss will affect the surviving partner. It is generous to pen some kind words about the deceased if you knew them, but avoid empty words which might smack of insincerity if they were not well known to you.

Black edged writing paper, as mentioned in the section on stationery, is reserved for letters of condolence, although it

66 Pavilion Road,
London
SW3 4DG
14th July 1999

Dear Charles,

I was extremely sorry to hear – via – Rupert Alexander – that your father had died.

It is, I fear, presumptuous of me to write – knowing you only a little – and express my sincere condolences. I do hope in your distress you will not allow any quarter to self-reproach. You could not have been more dutiful, and this alone must have been a great comfort to him.

I trust you will accept my sympathy and my feelings of considerable esteem.

Yours most sincerely,
Freddy de Rochefort

Figure 34: A letter of condolence to a friend whose father has passed away.

67

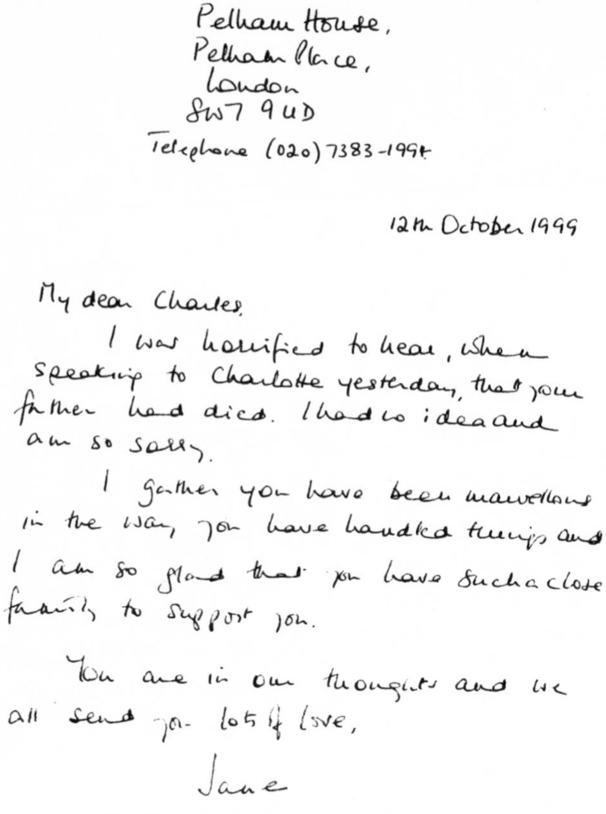

Pelham House,
Pelham Place,
London
SW7 9UD
Telephone (020) 7383-1994

12th October 1999

My dear Charles,

I was horrified to hear, when speaking to Charlotte yesterday, that your father had died. I had no idea and am so sorry.

I gather you have been marvellous in the way you have handled things and I am so glad that you have such a close family to support you.

You are in our thoughts and we all send you lots of love,

Jane

Figure 35: A letter of condolence from a distant family member.

is hardly ever used today. On the other extreme, the use of a brightly edged sheet of writing paper would be highly inappropriate. As mentioned previously, the use of a pre-printed 'In Sympathy' card is not considered appropriate and should never be used.

A close friend has kindly allowed me to reproduce a letter from a friend we share which was written after his father's recent death. I think you will agree that it is most tactfully and kindly written.

It is normal to reply personally to each letter of condolence as soon after the funeral as practicable. This may however take months if the deceased was a popular or public figure. An interim message on a pre-printed card may be sent, thanking people for their letters and flowers and informing them that you will reply personally to all of them soon.

Breaking difficult news

There are many occasions in life where a letter may be the perfect medium with which to break difficult news. Such an occasion might be to inform of an illness, the break-up of a marriage or partnership, financial problems, deciding to break off a friendship, or to 'come out', to name but a few. These letters, whilst drastically different in their content, are likely to cause similar shock and may cause an emotion not dissimilar to grieving on the part of the recipient. A letter is thus an ideal medium with which to allow difficult news to sink in, without requiring an immediate response on behalf of the reader. Unlike many of the subjects I deal with in this book, I will not attempt to give any examples of these kinds of letter but rather try to give some practical advice on things to include and things to avoid.

Naturally, the decision to make the step of writing will doubtless have entailed much reflection, if not years of trepidation. It may be the most difficult letter one ever writes. Without wishing to comment on the merits of such a disclosure, below are some of the considerations worth taking into account when penning such a letter.

- Remember that the reader may not understand anything about the subject. Attempt to reassure them, in
clear and concise language, what the news means both
for you and for them. Perhaps nothing has changed but
that they now have a more intimate knowledge of you.
Be honest with the reader. Reassure them that by
writing, you are showing your respect for them and
want to be honest with them.

- Spare your reader the 'gory' details. Because difficult
subjects are often those furthest from our minds, many
people have very unrealistic views of them. Be honest
but keep your reader's sensitivities in mind and try not
to go into unnecessary detail, particularly of something
like a terminal illness.

- If you remain happy despite this difficult news, tell
them. If not, tell them that too. The fact that you are
sharing this information shows that the reader is in
some way important to you and deserves a clear picture
of how this revelation is affecting you, not only them.

- Try not to attribute blame. Naturally, if you are
breaking off a friendship, the whole reason may be to
cast blame, yet it can be done without venom. Write
about how the situation or actions affect your feelings,
not simply dig up past hurt. A letter such as this is
emotive enough in itself and its purpose is not to
engender more heartache.

Chapter 8

The Thankyou Letter

Saying thank you, whether for the hospitality of a friend or for a gift received, is one of the mainstays of a polite society. By saying thank you, we acknowledge that the other has gone out of their way with an act of kindness. The magnitude of the act is really immaterial, it is always polite to communicate our thanks, and a letter is the perfect medium. With so many means of communication, whether telephone, email or fax, taking the time to pen a short note in your own hand conveys gratitude perfectly.

Reasons to write a letter of thanks are too numerous to deal with each individually, so the two examples of a gift and for a dinner party will be dealt with in this chapter. Examples will be given which may be modified for almost any occasion.

A thankyou letter should be written on the smaller paper which would normally be used for any social correspondence, and must always be handwritten. A4 or US letter size paper should be reserved for business correspondence unless the sheer volume warrants otherwise. Remember, a concise note which conveys your appreciation is always preferable to a gushing tome. The tone of such a letter depends entirely on how well you know the recipient and may be laced with a certain amount of humour if appropriate.

When should you write?

Diana, Princess of Wales was famed and appreciated as one who always penned thankyou letters, in her own hand, immediately on return from each engagement. The letter would arrive in the post the following day or the day after at the latest. Whilst this is not always convenient in the hustle and bustle of modern life, it highlights the importance of promptitude.

Leaving a letter too late can give the impression that the thanks are less sincere, or at least that they are less warmly felt. Remember that you are thanking another for an act of kindness; surely it is only polite to return the kindness by being prompt. Ideally then, a letter of thanks should be written and posted the day following the event or as soon thereafter as practicable.

Promptitude should not, however, be taken to extremes. There was a delightful story relayed to me by a friend whose mother received a letter from a friend whom she had entertained. The guest was invited to spend the weekend. As one seriously prone to forgetfulness, she thought that by penning the letter in advance and posting it on the way to her hosts' home, it would prevent her from forgetting to write upon her return. The factor she did not consider was the efficiency of the Royal Mail. Quite to her horror, her letter of thanks arrived on the Saturday morning of her weekend stay. Amusing to say the least. In fact both guest and host now tell the story with fondness, but at the time it was mortifying and could clearly be seen as a social *faux pas* of significant gravity.

To whom should you write?

Clearly, if the letter is in response to a gift, the giver is the obvious recipient. Yet, there are many other situations when a thankyou letter might be appropriate but whom to thank may be less obvious. Take a dinner party for example. Traditionally, the letter is always addressed to the hostess. This convention stands in traditional relationships; however relationships these days are far from traditional.

Today there are far fewer married couples about and it is just as likely that you might be hosted by sisters sharing a house, a group of flatmates, or indeed a gay couple. In such a situation, common sense prevails. If one of the hosts has clearly done all the preparation whilst the other, or others, were out at work on the day of the party, courtesy would dictate that the person who did the catering be addressed. If, on the other hand, the 'caterer' is less clear, it is perfectly acceptable to name each of the hosts, or simply the person who invited you, in the salutation. Always, however, acknowledge both or all of the hosts in the body of the note and make it clear that the evening was a success as a result of all concerned.

What should you say?

The text of the letter is naturally the most difficult element of the task at hand. Your own writing style, how well you know the addressee, use of humour... all of these considerations go into the production of a well received thankyou letter. There are those renowned for their well-written, sharp-witted and perceptive missives; becoming one of these people is certainly not impossible for any letter writer. For the budding author to do so, you simply need to develop a template which can be changed as the situation warrants. With a few letters under your belt, this template will become as natural as is the notion to put pen to paper after every dinner party.

Below are a few of the considerations you should make before writing a letter. The list is by no means exhaustive and other factors of the particular situation should always be taken into account. However, by making some methodical notes prior to writing the first draft, you are guaranteed to formulate a far better letter. As a rule of thumb, remember that nothing in any letter should appear frivolous; if a point or a person is mentioned, it should be for a reason and not seem gratuitous.

Comment on appropriateness

Naturally, the main reason for writing a thankyou letter is to thank. Such a letter would fail miserably in its purpose if it did not get across to the host that you are grateful for something. The simplest way of making this clear is to comment on the appropriateness of the event or of the gift. A lovely dinner party which served as an opportunity to meet a new friend, a surprise birthday party when the 'surprised' had thought all of his friends had forgotten, a thoughtful gift . . . noting the thoughtfulness behind someone's kindness is the key to showing you know what lengths were gone to in making the original gesture.

Always make the point of fussing over the host or gift giver to the point of making them feel good about the act of kindness they have 'committed'. When they have read the letter, they should think to themselves, "this letter is about me". Take this principle right to the edge without falling into the trap of gushiness.

Use of humour

As gratitude is the obvious reason for a letter, so too can humour be the most important factor in penning a good note. Its use can lighten the tone of an otherwise stuffy letter and can in some way continue the joviality of the event. There is a danger, however: humour can offend. Its use should be limited to letters to close friends or colleagues and should never appear frivolous. A rule of thumb: if the event or gift was fun or funny, use humour to describe it; if, however, a dinner, for example, was ghastly and an argument ensued between two guests, steer well clear of making light of the situation.

Mention all the hosts

As suggested earlier, mentioning all those who made the evening a success can be an important factor in modern social engagements where the 'hostess' is not the obvious choice of addressee. Make the effort to touch upon some way in which each contributed to the event. Avoid token mentions ("... and please pass on my thanks to your husband as well") as this may give entirely the opposite impression to that intended.

Mention other guests

Mentioning others present at a dinner can be a good way to flesh-out a letter and make it interesting. Comment on another guest's storytelling abilities or even attractiveness. Compliments that are conveyed back to people when conveyed through another often mean more than those said in person. New friends are often made at dinner parties, and how many lovers meet through mutual friends over a meal or at a party?

Apologise for any misbehaviour

In the writing of this chapter, a story was relayed to me about a young man who got so drunk at a wedding, he became rather too high-spirited. He and a friend began climbing the poles supporting the marquee and in so doing, toppled part of the structure. Whilst no doubt an entertaining spectacle, the Mother of the Bride was not even slightly amused. The following day, this unfortunate chap consulted his friend through the haze of a hangover to ask what he should do. Whilst thankyou letters are not normally required after a wedding (although not expressly inappropriate) it was suggested that he use this medium as an opportunity to apologise for his behaviour. Often apologising for bad behaviour takes the wind out of the sails of the person we have offended and a reconciliation is far more likely.

Whilst most will not go to such lengths to misbehave, staying too late at dinner might be a more common lack of consideration. Most hosts will appreciate the gesture of acknowledging such an incident and will probably not strike the writer from their list of future dinner guests.

Things to avoid

Stick to the task at hand. The purpose of a thankyou letter is not to extend a return invitation, ask for a favour, discuss business, criticise, or any other similar objective. The communication of such information in the body of a thankyou letter is always inappropriate. If another point needs to be made, a separate letter, or perhaps telephone call is required.

Thanking someone for the food is another thing which should always be avoided. By all means comment on lovely cooking, the imaginative menu, even for lovely strawberries in December, but not for the food. This is a fine line, but one of the inexact social mores of our society. It is considered gauche to be grateful for food as though one is in need of a free meal.

Methods of delivery

The rule of thumb here is that a letter of this type should always be posted unless delivering it by hand conveys something more. For example, if the thankyou letter is addressed to the wife of a colleague at work, it should never

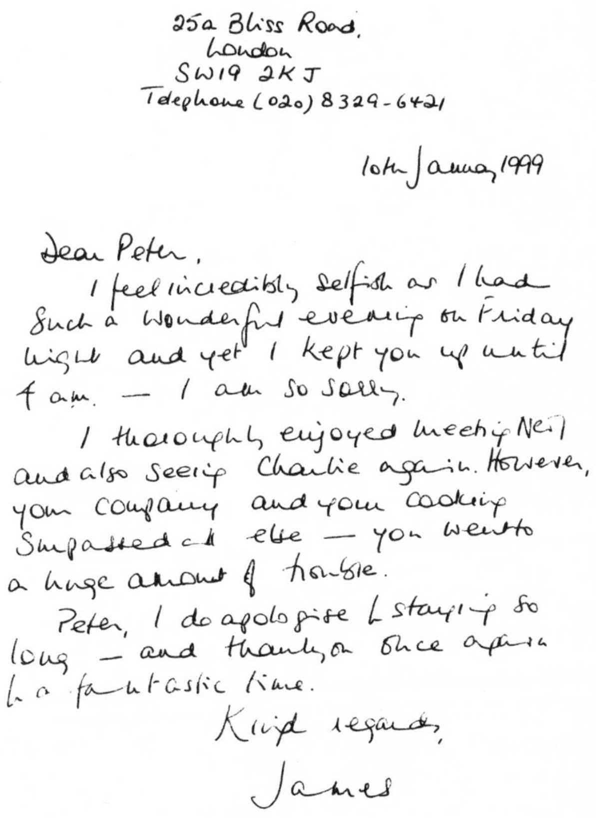

25a Bliss Road,
London
SW19 2KJ
Telephone (020) 8329-6421

10th January 1999

Dear Peter,
    I feel incredibly selfish as I had such a wonderful evening on Friday night and yet I kept you up until 4 a.m. — I am so sorry.

    I thoroughly enjoyed meeting Neil and also seeing Charlie again. However, your company and your cooking surpassed all else — you went to a huge amount of trouble.

    Peter, I do apologise L staying so long — and thank you once again L a fantastic time.
                    Kind regards,
                    James

Figure 36: Thankyou letter for a dinner party including an apology.

be taken to the office and put in the internal post. Whilst efficient, this might be seen by some as a mean attempt to save the cost of a stamp. It sends entirely the wrong signal from the intended message of gratitude. If however, hand-delivering a note to a neighbour shows that you have gone out of your way to ensure the letter arrives on a Sunday

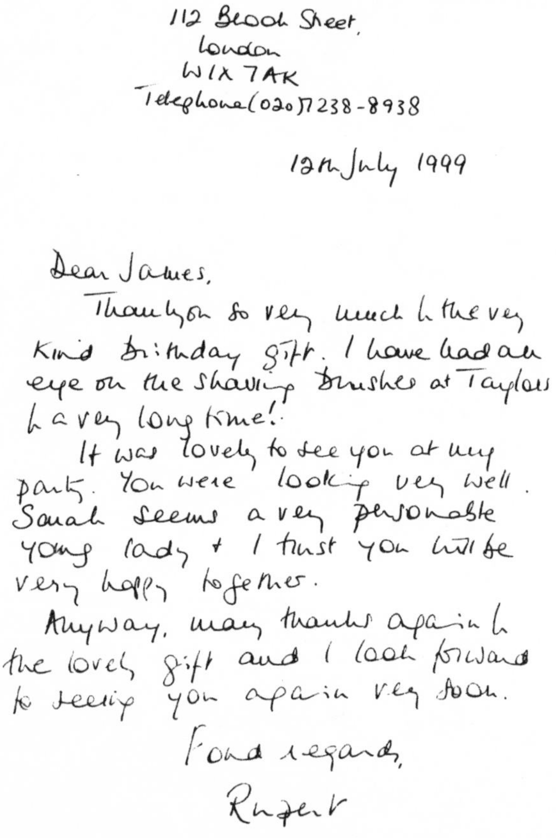

112 Brook Street,
London
W1X 7AK
Telephone (020) 7238-8938

12th July 1999

Dear James,

Thank you so very much for the very kind birthday gift. I have had an eye on the shaving brushes at Taylors for a very long time!

It was lovely to see you at my party. You were looking very well. Sarah seems a very personable young lady & I trust you will be very happy together.

Anyway, many thanks again for the lovely gift and I look forward to seeing you again very soon.

Fond regards,

Rupert

Figure 37: Thankyou letter for a gift.

morning after a Saturday supper for example, it clearly shows a heightened gratitude.

Likewise, with email, although it is an important method of sending thanks, it should be avoided except for very close friends. If you and the host have made some sort of agreement that you know one another well enough to dispense with the formality of thankyou letters, then email might be a suitable middle ground. Having a hand-written letter arrive in the post is, however, always appropriate and appreciated. If you do decide to deliver it by hand, it is common practice to write the words "By hand" in place of a postage stamp.

Chapter 9

===

The Begging Letter

Whether you are begging forgiveness, begging the question or begging for a loan, the 'begging letter' is asking another to make a decision about you. Are you worthy of that investment, or of forgiveness? This letter may be the first or indeed, only, impression, the reader has with which to make a decision about you. Make that impression count.

Asking for favours

A letter asking for a favour is an ideal way not to put the other party on the spot. It allows them to make a considered decision without feeling any pressure from hearing your breath at the other end of the telephone, or worse yet from your puppy-dog facial expression. Below is a letter asking for a loan from someone who has previously made the offer. Its format can be altered to fit any situation.

Apologies and making up with people

There are many times in life when our actions or words go just that little bit too far and offend another. This other may be a friend, business colleague, relative or neighbour.

80

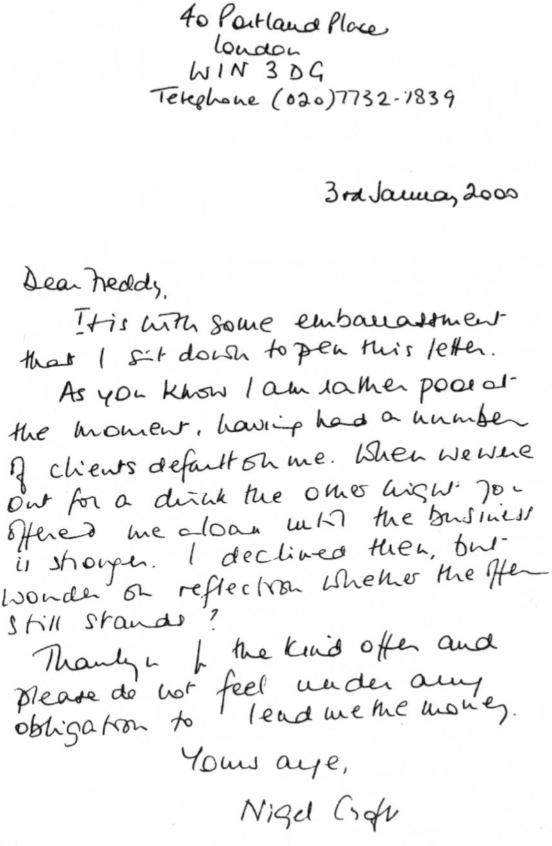

40 Portland Place
London
WIN 3 DG
Telephone (020)7732-1839

3rd January, 2000

Dear Teddy,

It is with some embarrassment that I sit down to pen this letter.

As you know I am rather poor at the moment, having had a number of clients default on me. When we were out for a drink the other night you offered me a loan until the business is stronger. I declined then, but wonder on reflection whether the offer still stands?

Thankyou for the kind offer and please do not feel under any obligation to lend me the money.

Yours aye,

Nigel Croft

Figure 38: Letter to a friend asking for a loan.

Nevertheless, writing a quick note to say you are sorry can go a very long way to rebuilding bridges regardless of who the offended might be or your previous relationship with them. A letter, even more than a telephone call, underlines the importance you give to your apology and acknowledges the distress you may have caused.

81

In the same way that trying to make up with someone can rebuild bridges, apologising before the event can be a useful tool in building bridges. For example, we were planning a party at home which was going to be both loud and late. Couple this with the fact that we lived in a terraced house and the newly arrived next-door neighbours had a new-born baby. Having a party and keeping them up all night in their first week in the house would not have been very neighbourly, so we wrote the following letter.

66 Bolingbroke Grove,
London
SW11 6HE
Telephone (020) 7228-6210

12th December 1999

Dear new neighbours,

Welcome to the neighbourhood! Just to let you know that we are having a Christmas party this Friday night and wanted to apologise in advance for the noise. We will try to confine the party and hopefully you will not be disturbed too much.

We'd be delighted if you wanted to drop by. An invitation is enclosed.

Kind regards,

Robert, et al'

Figure 39: Letter of apology for a noisy party.

I will not attempt to give further examples of letters of apology as the situations are too numerous. Simply keep in mind that you are writing to apologise and not to lay any blame on anyone but yourself. "I'm sorry, but..." is not the sort of phrase we are looking for here. If there is a situation which needs to be addressed, by all means bring it up, but do not attempt to excuse your behaviour because of a situation. If you are writing to apologise you must at least admit that you have behaved in a way which is less than desirable – admit it and move on.

Renewing friendships

All too often we lose touch with friends these days, and more is the pity. Assuming there has not been a significant falling-out, renewing an old friendship can be a rewarding and enjoyable experience for both parties. Below is a letter which exemplifies the kinds of things you might say in such a letter.

Asking yourself to stay

Asking yourself to stay can be the hardest favour to ask. Yet, at the same time, staying with friends as you are passing through an area for another reason can be a great opportunity to renew a friendship. That said, we all know the old adage that house guests, like fish, begin to smell after three days. Keep those wise words in the back of your mind as you pen this letter and you will not go wrong. If you are going to be in an area for an extended period, either write to two separate sets of friends or make plans to stay in a hotel. You can always change your plans if you find you are getting along well with your hosts and they make a genuine offer to have you for longer.

45 Earl's Court Square,
London
SW5 9PG
Telephone (020) 373-2581

Dear Damian,

No doubt this letter will come as a bit of a blast from the past! I was at a wedding recently and your name came up in the conversation.

Since moving to London, I've rather lost touch with friends from the regiment; it's something I wish had not happened. That said, I was hoping we could get together to relive old times.

I'm working for a merchant bank near Moorgate, so if you're in the area, why don't we link up for a drink?

Give me a ring at home or during the day at the office.

Hope to hear from you soon.

Yours aye,

Charlie

Figure 40: Letter to renew a friendship. Pick on the good times and explicitly ask for a reply or suggest a social meeting of some sort.

45 Earl's Court Square,
London
SW5 9 PG
Telephone (020)373-2581

Dear Bill + Mary,

I trust this letter finds you well
and enjoying the wonderful summer.

I am coming to Edinburgh for the
Festival this year. I'll be in touch on 12th
and 13th August but may stay for the
weekend as well. I was wondering
if you don't have anyone else staying,
would it be too much of an imposition
to use your spare room for those nights
I realise this is very short notice,
so please don't feel under any
obligation.

Many thanks in advance + I
look forward to hearing from you
soon.

Kind regards,
Charlie

Figure 41: Letter inviting yourself to stay.

85

Chapter 10

====

Letters of Affection

This section only deals in part with letters to lovers. Others of this kind may include, but are not limited to, children, family members and close friends. The content of such letters is wide and varied but the structure and semantics follow certain conventions.

Letters to children

Letters to children can be a lot of fun and I very much enjoy the limited amount of correspondence I have with my nieces and nephews, although much of it these days is by email over the Internet. Yet, as a child when staying away from home, it was always a treat to receive post from my sisters or parents, particularly when in the company of other children. Have fun with letters to children.

'Mail call' at summer camp in Canada was always a favourite time of day, and many older siblings who had been through the experience themselves were very good at 'stitching-up' their younger brothers. Dousing letters in perfume was always a favourite, and postcards with naughty pictures were always a favourite which gave the recipient a certain amount of 'street cred' in the eyes of their peers.

Have fun with letters to children, be they at relatives for the summer or away at school. Avoid being condescending or simply relating dull news. It is difficult enough to get children to write back, so ask lots of questions which they may at least feel obliged to answer.

The use of the styles 'Master' and 'Esq.' for young men away at school is dealt with in some depth on page 31.

Letters to lovers – when things go wrong

There are times when things do go wrong in relationships. At such times, we may try several tactics to deal with the rift, from running away (either figuratively or literally), to being grown up and facing the person. If neither appeals, the other option is to put your thoughts on paper, an option which has two distinct advantages. Firstly, it allows you to get your thoughts together in an orderly fashion and also lets you take time over the writing of such a letter. If you were to attempt to say the same things in person you would be likely to forget an important point, or worse yet, say something you do not mean. The second advantage to writing a letter in this kind of situation is that it allows the news to sink in on the part of the reader, without them being expected to respond immediately. If they become emotional, they do not have to worry about baring their soul in a situation they may be totally unprepared for.

Below I have included a letter written in just such a situation. The names have naturally been changed to protect the innocent (and the guilty).

110 Eaton Square
London
SW1

Dear Jane,

I've been trying to have a chat with you about our friendship since your birthday but the time has never seemed right.

You're an intuitive woman, so no doubt you've had an inkling of how much you've come to mean to me. No falling in love crap but I was certainly 'in like', if that makes any sense. From the very beginning you said you didn't want to get into a relationship and just wanted to remain friends. Knowing that was very difficult h me, so I began consciously trying to stop myself be coming any fonder of you than I already was.

I admit though that I still think of you although I am sure I have blown it between us. Jane, I wish you all the best with your new man. He's very lucky and I hope things work out and you're very happy.

With kindest regards,

Roger

Figure 42: Letter to a lover when things have gone wrong. Avoid recrimination and take responsibility for your own actions. Above all, be totally frank and honest.

Chapter 11

The Letter as a Diary

There is some value for your own sake in writing when travelling. Many travellers keep a journal or travelogue which they can re-read as their journey progresses. Another option however, is to write and post letters, either to an intimate or to yourself with instructions that the letters should remain unopened.

I cannot give much advice here, nor could I attempt to give any examples. All I can really advise is that these letters are the sort that will no doubt be read by you time and again in future years. It is worth including information not only about the progress of your geographical journey but also about your personal and emotional journey. It is the latter information which will be of far greater interest to you as you look back on times of travel and personal development in years to come.

Chapter 12

Fax and Email

You may well say that a letter sent through a facsimile machine (commonly known as a fax), and electronic mail (commonly known as email), are simply methods of delivery. To a great extent that is true. However, as I mentioned earlier, in some cases the medium becomes the message. It is thus very important to ensure that by employing these mediums, you do not send an altogether inappropriate message.

Faxes

As information technology becomes more advanced and indeed more available to the ordinary person, the fax machine is becoming slightly less used than it was five years ago. It is, however, still very useful for certain things and I doubt its use will disappear forever for some time yet. Now, with the advent of plain paper fax machines, we have moved away from the curly paper which turns brown after a few weeks and documents can be kept without having to be photocopied onto suitable paper.

When sending faxes from home, it is unlikely that you will need to use what has become known as a cover sheet. That is, one page sent at the beginning of a document which gives all the pertinent information on the sender, recipient, company, date, number of pages, telephone numbers, etc. It is quite permissible to type "BY FAX AND POST" in bold letters under the recipient's address block on a letter of a business nature. If it is not a typewritten business letter, do ensure the document you are sending will get to the right person on the other end. It should always be clearly marked with at least the following information:

- name of recipient;
- name of sender;
- number of pages (i.e. "page 1 of 3");
- a telephone number to ring if there is a problem with transmission.

There are also several types of pre-printed 'sticky' notes which can be used for faxes which might negate the need for a cover sheet.

Email

Email is another form of communication which has become widely used in the past couple of years. It is getting to the stage where we are bombarded with more electronic junk mail than we are with direct mail at home. That said, its advent allows us the opportunity to correspond almost instantaneously and have a reply, often within minutes. Even William Dockwra and his Penny Post of twelve deliveries per day could not keep up.

If you decide that email is the medium you choose to convey your thoughts, you might consider using some of the more popular Internet chat symbols and abbreviations to illustrate your mood. These are made using standard keyboard punctuation keys:

91

:)	Smile	:-)	Smile with nose
;)	Wink	:-P	Sticking out tongue
;-)	Wink (with nose)	{}	Hug
:o)	Another smile	:(	Frown
:D	Smile/laughing/big grin	:'(	Crying
:*	Kiss	:-&	Tongue-tied
:-|	Grim face	:X	My lips are sealed

Chapter 13

======

Conducting Business
From Home

Many of us in this day and age do much of our work from home. In this section I am not attempting to teach anyone how to run a home-based business or indeed how to run an office. What I am hoping to achieve is to expand on some of the more prevalent letters any of us might be asked to write, which have an impact on our own or others' business lives, whether we work from home or not. Typically, the sort of letters we might write out of the office which have an impact in the office are references, letters of application and finally, letters of resignation. Each will be discussed in greater detail below, but first let us look at some of the basics.

Letters of this kind will generally be the only ones which we do not write on our own writing paper. They should ideally be typewritten on white (or another suitably muted colour) A4 or US letter size paper. Each business seems to have its own layout of choice, but there are two basic letter formats which we will consider – others are simply a variation on the theme. The first, semi-blocked layout, has the address block on the left margin, followed by indented lines of text without spaces between paragraphs; the signatory block is normally lined up with the sender's address block just right of the centre of the page. The second, fully-blocked layout, sees both the sender's and addressee's block, as well as the signatory block aligned with the left margin; lines of text are not indented but a space is left between paragraphs. The examples on the following pages are in both layouts and are annotated for clarity.

You should endeavour to know your reader to enable you to write to a person rather than a position and negate the need for opening address or salutation such as, "Dear Sir," unless the formality of the letter dictates such a salutation. The table below gives advice on when the different salutations and subscriptions, or methods of signing off, should be used.

Salutations		
Formal	Sir	Now outdated except in very formal circumstances or when writing to the editor of a newspaper.
	Dear Sir	When writing to someone who is unknown and where formality is required. The combination, "Dear Sir/Madam" should never be used.
Business	Dear Mr Smith	Perfectly acceptable for most business letters. Neither overly formal nor familiar.
	Dear Mary Jones	Less formal and negates the need to find out a woman's preferred style (Mrs. Miss, Ms., etc.).
Social	Dear Harry	The use of "My" before "Dear" is appropriate only if a tone of affection is desired. Be careful, it can seem pompous.

Subscriptions		
Formal	I remain (or I am), Your Grace, Most Reverend Sir, My Lord, Mr President, Mr Chairman, Sir, Madam, etc. Yours faithfully (or Yours truly)	These very formal styles of ending letters have become almost obsolete, except in the armed forces. If required, such a subscription should only be used with the salutation "Sir".
	Yours faithfully	The normal salutation in a formal letter beginning "Dear Sir".
Business	Yours faithfully (or Yours truly)	Again, used only with the salutation, "Dear Sir".
	Yours sincerely	To a business addressee you know or to whom you have spoken and who is named in the salutation (eg. "Dear Mr Smith").
Social	Sincerely	Generally only used in a semi-formal social letter such as a letter of condolence or to someone whom you do not know well.
	Yours	Usually used with a very close friend or lover. If used outside this kind of relationship (ie. in a business environment) it can seem very cold. Its use is thus not recommended.
	Yours aye	A very traditional salutation used widely between officers in the armed forces. Literally, "Yours always".
	With kind regards, With fond regards, With love, Ever yours, Lots of love, etc.	The combinations are endless and denote differing levels of both acquaintance and fondness. The choice is yours.
	With love from	Generally used only when writing to children; often seen on letters from grandparents.

Job applications

Whether you are applying for your first job, exploring a second career or even looking for work experience, a cunningly worded letter will no doubt be your first task. This letter may or may not be hand-written. More commonly it will be produced on a word processor but the same rules of care and attention to the correct way of writing apply, as they do to the personal hand-written letter. There is a real art to writing this very different kind of letter. The art is to tell your audience enough to get them interested, but not too much that they don't need to interview you. This technique of skilful, minimalist phrasing is known as a 'hook'. Remember that writing a letter to a prospective employer is the equivalent of a salesman's 'cold call', the only real difference being that what you are selling is yourself.

Before we even consider the text of your letter, there are several things you can do to get your letter to the right person, then read and acted upon rather than simply being thrown in the bin:

- Use your contacts. The cliché 'It's not what you know but who you know' is as true today as it ever was. With the exception of my time in the Forces, every job I have ever had (including the writing of this book) came from some sort of personal connection. If you set your mind to it, you can probably think of someone (a friend of a friend of a friend, even) in almost any industry. The person may well not be in a position to hire you, but in most cases will be willing to meet you to tell you what they do; if you impress them at this stage, they may well put you in touch with someone who can hire you.
- Presentation says a great deal about you. Make sure that your letter is neat, correctly formatted, clear and

readable, typewritten, and free from coffee stains or other such unsightly smudges. It sounds obvious, but you would be amazed at the number of letters and CVs which landed on my desk when I was hiring people in the City which were scrawled on tatty bits of paper. Gone are the days of handwriting a letter to prove to a prospective employer that you can write. Use modern methods for modern job hunting.

- Get your intended reader's name, title and address right. Unless you are dealing with a very small company where the managing director is going to answer the telephone, a quick chat with the receptionist will gain significant results. Make sure you get the spelling of the person's name correct, the right office address (some companies work from several different buildings in the same area) and try to find the title the person likes to use (e.g. Miss or Ms).

The timing of your application

Consider the timing of your application. Something I've always done when sending a letter of this type is to post it between Monday and Wednesday but never between Thursday and Sunday. In so doing, my letters never land on a prospective employer's desk on a Monday or Friday. Many of us can relate to that Monday morning, first-day-back-at-work-with-a-mountain-of-post feeling; conversely on Fridays, our minds are often on the coming weekend. In my mind, people are potentially less receptive to being won over on either of these days. I also try to time follow up telephone calls for 11am so that I catch people after they have settled in for the day but before lunch. I should stress that these ideas are only quirks of mine and I have no evidence (scientific or empirical) that they make the blindest bit of difference. That said, I would strongly recommend that you don't consider the application process to be complete when you put the stamp on the envelope and pop it in the post.

Now to the text. The key here is to keep in mind your purpose: you want an interview. We now enter the argument between the two schools of thought in operation here. One is the traditionally worded compliant and less assertive approach, the other is the rather more pushy, approach. Rather than trying to explain further, examples of the two are included below.

Adapt one of these two approaches to your intended audience. The first might be better for more traditional letters of application (which might cover a CV) to an advertised job; the latter would be more suited to a 'cold call' letter or where an application asks you to demonstrate certain qualities. I have even seen letters in response to appointments advertisements which list qualities in two columns, such as:

You seek someone with experience of....	My background in… is directly suited to…
You need someone who is…	I am….
You want someone with…	I have…

       …and so on.

This style of letter can be a very effective tool; I know of at least one friend who impressed an employer enough to 'hook' them into interviewing him. The technique of 'matching' needs with skills can also be woven into the body of a 'normal' letter.

I mentioned earlier the art of minimalist writing. That is, the idea that you want to tell your reader enough to whet their appetite and compel them to interview you. This can often be done with the use of subtly worded sentences which have the same effect as name-dropping in conversa-

23 Eaton Square
LONDON
SW1H 2BE

Tel/Fax: (020) 7555-1212
Mobile: (07958) 555 111
Email: simon.pilk@virgin.net

Jane Grant
The Coffee Company
11 Munster Road
LONDON
SW6 3PG   2 September 1999

As The Coffee Company takes over the UK, no doubt you are attempting to create brand identity in your advertising. It is well known that brand identity is often linked to a particular voice. As such, I believe your strategy should include a 'voice of The Coffee Company' for radio and television advertising. I would like to be that voice.

Originally from Seattle, I have been acquainted with The Coffee Company for many years and am a loyal customer. I am also a voice-over artist with a versatile mid-Atlantic accent. A perfect mix for The Coffee Company identity!

By employing me directly, you would avoid the fees normally charged by an expensive voice agent.

I am very keen to work with you and would be delighted to meet for a chat. I have enclosed a copy of my demo tape for your consideration. Thank you for your attention and I look forward to hearing from you soon.

Yours sincerely

Simon Pilkington

/Encl.

Figure 43: Example of a semi-blocked layout. Lines of text are indented and the writer's address block and signature block are aligned with the date just right of centre. A rather more pushy approach to the one which follows.

23 Eaton Square
LONDON
SW1H 2BE

Tel/Fax: (020) 7555-1212
Mobile: (07958) 555-111
Email: simon.pilk@virgin.net

Ms Rebecca Jones
The Movie Production Company
323 Wardour Street
LONDON
W1V 5BR

15 September 1999

Dear Ms Jones

I am very keen to break into a second career in broadcasting,
with a particular interest in the production of commercials. My
background as a merchant banker is probably rather different
from the majority of those who apply to your company, however,
I believe I have the skills and discipline required to be successful
in the industry.

I am seeking an entry level production position with an
established company. My wealth of varied experience, coupled
with sound organisational and administrative skills, could be of
great use to your company. I would relish a chance to prove my
worth to you.

I have enclosed a copy of my CV for your perusal. I would be
most willing to meet to discuss any possibilities with you. Thank
you for your consideration.

Yours sincerely,

Simon Pilkington

/Encl.

Figure 44: A traditional letter of application. The fully blocked
layout aligns all text with the left margin. Lines of text are not
indented but a space is left between paragraphs.

From: Lieutenant General Sir James Russell KCB

Re: Captain Neil Forester MBE

To Whom It May Concern:

Captain Neil Forester worked closely for me as a member of my personal staff for two years until May 1996. During this period I got to know him very well, travelling thousands of miles together. He was responsible for arranging my daily programme and other personal staff work.

Professionally, Neil coped admirably with a formidable workload, displaying excellent organisational skills, a logical mind, great tact and diplomacy, and a delightful sense of humour. He was utterly loyal and dependable, and quickly gained both the liking and respect of the rest of my much more senior staff. He thrives on hard work and has plenty of stamina as well as a finely tuned eye for detail. Cheerful, co-operative and flexible, he has a good mind and argues his corner with conviction but, regardless of the outcome of debate, accepts the result with great equanimity. He is sustained by firmly held Christian beliefs.

In summary I have been very well served by Neil Forester, hold him in high esteem and can recommend him without reservation to any employer.

J. R. St J. RUSSELL
Lieutenant General
August 1999

Figure 45: An example reference which may be used over again. It should include the referee's name and a date but need not include a return address or telephone number unless the person would be difficult to track down. References may be hand-written.

tion. I have a friend who, in a letter of application for an internal promotion, needed to demonstrate experience but was not allowed to use examples more than three years old. To get around this, he started a sentence, "Building on my past experience in the Foreign Office...." It turned out to be just enough to set him apart from the hundreds of other applications and got him an interview.

The following are some useful sentences for beginning and ending letters of application. Don't follow them strictly but use them as a guide and alter them to suit your audience.

Beginnings:

"Thank you for your letter of 26 July 1999 shortlisting me for the position of...."

"Further to my letter of 18 September 1999, I thought you would wish to be aware that..."

"I write in response to your advertisement in The Times for the position of..."

"I read with interest your advertisement in yesterday's Telegraph. I am seeking..."

"Having recently left the Royal Navy where I served for the past seven years..."

Endings:

"Thank you for your consideration and I look forward to hearing from you soon."

"Please find enclosed a copy of my CV for your perusal."

"Please do not hesitate to contact me on the above number if you require any further information."

References

References are generally given in one of two ways. The first case is when you will be asked by a prospective employer for the name and address of a referee; this requires no action on your part except a quick note or telephone call to confirm the willingness of the person to act as a referee. This is only polite and should always be done in good time to warn the referee of an impending inquiry. It also gives you good warning if they intend to be less than complimentary in their reference, in which case you would be well advised to go to someone else.

Asking for a reference

The second case is when you ask a former employer for a general reference. These references are very useful, either to include with your CV or to have on hand to show an employer at your interview. They are normally addressed "To Whom it May Concern" and can be used over and over again. When photocopying these valuable references, make sure the copies are always clear of marks and cleanly presented so that future attempts to photocopy do not result in a grey and indistinct version of the original.

Apart from simply being polite, using a letter to ask for a reference gives you the added opportunity to help the referee in the writing of the reference. By noting some of the points you would like them to mention in the letter (perhaps reminding them of certain instances where you feel you performed particularly well) you will give them the ammunition for good examples.

Giving a reference

In writing a reference for someone else, you should only include commendatory information. If you have serious misgivings about a person's ability to fulfil a role for which they are being considered, be honest and respond to their request with a short note saying that you do not feel able to give a reference on this occasion.

103

In the writing, do not be overly gushing but give a clear picture of the person and their abilities. Mention the capacity in which you know them (including a brief outline of their duties if appropriate and not obvious) and for how long. The reference should not be longer than one side except in exceptional cases and should be signed and dated. Unlike the letter of application itself, a reference may be hand-written.

Resignation

In a culture where we are told that changing careers at least three times in our working life is normal, a letter of resignation is something we are all likely to write. That said, there may be other occasions where a similar letter is necessary, if only taking ourselves off a local parish council or resigning from a voluntary post. In any case, it is worth getting such a letter right, as there is room here for much misinterpretation.

In writing a letter of resignation, it is important to avoid making irrevocable statements in case one has cause to meet the person at a future date in another context. Avoid recriminations, criticism of your employer or the way they run the business. Above all, keep your personal, negative feelings out. If you have enjoyed your employment, and will miss your colleagues, by all means mention that this is the case.

My firm advice is keep your letter of resignation as short as possible and include only that information which you wish to appear on your personal file with the company. When personally handing in such a letter, you will no doubt be given ample opportunity to explain your reasons, if they are not already apparent. The two main things which you must get right when writing a letter of resignation are the correct addressee and your notice period – the rest is padding. I have included an example of a letter I wrote recently to illustrate the brevity to which I recommend you aspire.

23 Eaton Square
LONDON
SW1H 2BE

Tel/Fax (020) 7555-3212
Mobile: (07958) 555 111
email: neil.forester@virgin.net

Jane Pilkington
Director of Corporate Communications
Swiss Bank
12 Broadgate
LONDON
EC2N 3PG

2 September, 1999

Dear Jane

It is with regret that I tender my resignation as Operations Manager of the Corporate Communications Department at Swiss Bank.

I have very much enjoyed my time with the bank and my departure is for purely personal reasons. I have very much appreciated the trust I have been given, but feel that leaving now will, in the fullness of time, be beneficial to both the Department and myself.

My last day with the bank will be 1 October 1999 in accordance with my contractual notice period.

Yours sincerely,

Neil Forester

Figure 46: A letter of resignation should avoid criticism of your employer. Ensure you write to the right person and include your notice period.

Chapter 14

════

Writing to Your Member of Parliament

Let us assume there are two reasons you would write to your MP. First, to praise them for the way they voted in Parliament or for some other noteworthy action on their part. Secondly, we might write to complain or 'encourage' them to support our cause. In the first case, you probably need little advice on how to get your point across. I would submit that it is the second of the two letters which may need further exploration. An MP once told me that for every letter his office receives, they assume that there are six others in the constituency who think or feel the same way but do not bother to write; all the more reason to write and get across the point of view of all seven of you.

If you have got to the stage of writing to your MP, the issue at hand has no doubt become somewhat emotive. Needless to say, you are not happy with something the Government as a whole is doing or with something your MP as an individual is up to. Your intention may be to complain or you may simply wish to put pressure on your MP to vote a certain way in the House on an upcoming issue.

Like any letter, the key here is brevity. A Member of Parliament will no doubt have a staff who will help him or her sift through correspondence from their constituents but by being brief and to the point, you will have a much greater chance of having your letter read and acted upon by the MP. Imagine that the letter is only read once, and for an average of three seconds. What you are seeking is immediate and understandable expression of your intent. Let us look at some guidelines:

- Do keep your letter brief – if there is a requirement to include any 'proof' do so with the use of appendices attached to a covering letter.
- Do stick to one issue – a 'scatter-gun' approach to Government policy is difficult for anyone to defend and will not get you a clear response.
- Do ensure that you are writing to the correct MP – you can find out who your MP is by ringing the House of Commons Information Office on (020) 7219 4272 or if you are connected to the Internet you can use the 'Constituency Locata' on the House of Commons website. By entering your postcode at the following site, you will be given the name of your MP and constituency, including contact details for him or her, with an email address if they have one: http://www.locata.co.uk/commons
- Do be businesslike – your letter should ideally be typed and laid out in an acceptable format.
- Don't ask the MP to do something which it is not within their remit to do – have you exhausted enquiries through the appropriate government department first?
- Don't attack the MP's character – personal slights will not help your cause.
- Do ask your MP for a response – if you are clear and logical in your argument and have asked for a response, you are more than likely to get one (even if it is not the one you were hoping for).

Letters to Members of Parliament should be addressed to them either at their Constituency Office or at the House of Commons. The envelope should be addressed thus:

> Mary Smith, MP
> House of Commons
> Westminster
> London SW1A 0AA

Normal correspondence to an MP, either at the House of Commons or at the Constituency Office, requires normal postage. If, however, you are sending a petition, mark the envelope "Petition to the House of Commons" (or House of Lords) and it may be sent free of postage.

Chapter 15

====

Methods of Delivery

Post note ...

Now that you have written your letter, choose postage or delivery. If sending the letter abroad, or enclosing something with your letter that makes it warrant more than a first class stamp (never second – it implies that you do not value the speed of your own communication), ensure you have the correct postage. Imagine the mood of the recipient if he or she has to pay the postage due for your letter, before they even read it.

At this stage one might have cause to be grateful that we live in an age with an effective postal system.

From Persia —

The establishment of a means of communication between people in different parts of a country seems to be one of the earliest marks of a developing civilisation. These civilisations began to intercommunicate over distance wholly by using messengers who carried simple oral dispatches. This was understandably an inherently unreliable means of communicating. Messengers might fall victim to hostility or injury, or simply forget an important part of the message with which they had been entrusted. It was quickly discovered that this medium was of little or no value in the case of important dispatches or those which required secrecy. Written signs were thus employed which the recipient could understand and these primitive missives were often 'written' on the body of the messenger. In fact, the secrecy issue became of such importance that remarkable methods were resorted to. There is the story related by Herodotus (who lived in Greece from 484-425 BC) which was to shave the head of a messenger and to impress the message on the bald scalp. The messenger would then wait until enough hair had grown back to hide the writing before attempting delivery. At the other end, the head would be shaved to reveal the note. A rather more complex procedure than opening even the most stubborn modern plastic self-assessment tax return cover.

Hence, sending messages was limited to a very few and history tells us that the first 'letters' were solely on business of State. The Old Testament gives some very early references to letters. The first letter is credited to Queen Jezebel, wife of King Ahab. The Second Book of Kings tells us the story of Naaman, the Aramean general, who carried a letter from his King to the King of Israel in about 900 BC. The letter read, "With this letter I am sending my servant Naaman to you so that you may cure him of his leprosy."(NIV).* So even from early days, whilst often borne by official messengers, letters had a very personal message. Later, in the book of Esther, another King, Xerxes, sent yet another personal letter to every part of his kingdom. His wife had refused to obey him so he decreed in his letter that, "every man should be ruler over his own household". (NIV) Poor King Xerxes.

Footnote: *New International Version Holy Bible.

The first reference to anything like the postal system which we know today is down to Cyrus the Great who ruled Persia from 557–529 BC. In keeping with his great empire, Cyrus was a great road-builder and used these roads to develop a regular riding post throughout Persia. There were stations along these roads, positioned a day's horse ride from one another, where men and horses were always at the ready. It was an elaborate system which must have mightily impressed our friend Herodotus who commented that, "Nothing in the world is borne so swiftly as messages by the Persian couriers". In fact, his famous words are now carved on the façade of the New York Post Office, which paints a poetic picture of the postman: "Neither snow nor heat nor gloom of night stays these couriers from the swift completion of their appointed rounds". What would he have to say of email we wonder?

It is said of the Greeks that private correspondence scarcely existed prior to 600 BC. Subsequently, however, special messengers or runners were employed to carry State messages and the Greek postal system was born. Greek legends are full of romantic stories of the exploits of postmen. One of these messengers, Phidippides, has been immortalised by the story of running from Athens to Sparta, a distance of 125 miles, in two days. Whilst we might reject the story of a single runner as impossible, even the speed of those who carried the message in various stages is incredible. The devotion of this postman who carried the news of the defeat at Marathon to his leaders in Athens has again been immortalised in history; at the very moment that he had discharged his duty in delivering the message, he dropped dead from exhaustion.

The Chinese too had an early postal system, yet principally it seems to have been designed to deliver news to the distant and less populated districts. Marco Polo, the celebrated

Venetian traveller who visited China in the 13th century described their system as being very similar to that of the Persian couriers. It consisted of some 25,000 relay stations but was not available to non-Imperial business.

The Romans, however, were the first to combine the Greek romance of the post with Persian efficiency. Augustus Caesar, Emperor of Rome from 27 BC, established a postal system which, by AD 200, delivered some private mail. Whilst the establishment of anything like the modern postal system, charged with the delivery of personal correspondence is clouded with much obscurity, it is likely due to the Roman occupation of Britain that this country was to see its first post. Like the Persians, the Roman road was built with communication as its foremost purpose. From the most famous of Roman roads, the Appian Way, to the fifth of the great five which crossed the alpine passes to Gaul, Germany and Britain, roads were the cornerstone of the Empire. The first posts were like the Greek runners but under Augustus, good roads meant these running postmen could be replaced by horses. Roads were now measured and marked by the erection of stones at a distance of a thousand paces, or the Roman 'mille', and post stages were erected at the natural end of a day's journey. Although the Roman post was designed to serve the official needs of the Empire, it was increasingly used for private correspondence.

– to the Royal Mail

When Roman legions marched along the Dover road for the last time, they left Britain and indeed most of Europe, without a postal system. Europe, for the most part, drifted back to barbarism. No organised system of posts was reestablished in Britain until the reign of James I, prior to which anything which existed was due purely to private enterprise. Originally, both private and State letters were sent by messenger. By the close of the 15th century and early in the 16th, we find the words, "Haste, Post, Haste" written on the back of private letters. We can then assume that some sort of established postal system was in existence which was not confined to government correspondence alone.

In 1657, Cromwell said to Parliament, "there are many dangerous and wicked designs which have been and are daily contrived against the peace and welfare of this Commonwealth, the intelligence whereof cannot be well communicated but by letter of escript". He was obviously well aware of the power of communication through the postal system of his day and was keen to retain the monopoly which was first created by Elizabeth I and then James I of England (James VI of Scotland). These two monarchs had banned the transmission of domestic letters by any other means than government approved postmen; Cromwell was evidently keen to maintain this monopoly.

In 1680, William Dockwra founded the London Penny Post as a direct competitor to the government postal system. He charged a penny for a letter to be delivered within London through a network of receiving stations set up in coffee houses and taverns. There were hourly collections and 4-8 deliveries in most parts of the city. In the business districts there were as many as 12 deliveries each day. Customers could thus send a letter and receive a reply in the same day. In the end, Dockwra was fined for operating his Penny Post because it encroached on the State monopoly. Additionally, he was ordered to pay compensation to the government even though they were to benefit from his forward thinking and dynamic business sense. The Post Office of the day took over and continued to run Dockwra's 400 collection points and the London Penny Post continued to run well into the 19th century.

It is an interesting coincidence that the number of letters written seems to have dramatically increased with the institution of the Penny Post. I say coincidence because what may seem an obvious conclusion that people did not bother to write to one another before there was an inexpensive method of transmission of mail may not be the only factor. Indeed, around the same time, workers were beginning to send their children to school and literacy rates were thus dramatically increasing. In the days before the Penny Post, it may have been that many people simply could not write. Yet it seems that our quest to communicate has increased dramatically in the relatively short period since 1680. The Royal Mail handled 17,500 million units of post in 1994/1995. It is almost impossible to say how many of these units are actual letters of the type we are interested in and how many are business letters, or more prevalent, 'junk mail'. It would be interesting to know if the advent of email and other methods of communicating have caused a decline in the number of handwritten letters which are sent each year. It is unlikely that we will ever know.

Appendix

===

Correct forms of address

If you are seeking the correct way to address a person of rank or status, whether it is in the Armed Services, the Church or the aristrocracy, I have found the most invaluable source of reference to be *Debrett's Correct Form*. Here, the manner of address, whether it is in person, on an envelope or an invitation, is mentioned in great detail. Below, however, I have tabulated some of the most commonly used titles and their various forms.

Name	How to address the person on the envelope	How to address the person in a letter
Duke	The Duke of Smithshire	Dear Duke/ Dear Duke of Smithshire
Duchess	The Duchess of Smithshire	Dear Duchess/Dear Duchess of Smithshire
Eldest son of duke usually takes his father's second title as a courtesy title	Marquess of Smithshire	Dear Lord Smithshire

Younger son of a duke	The Lord James Smithshire (family name)	Dear Lord James
Wife of younger son of a duke	The Lady James… (family name)	Dear Lady James
Daughter of a duke	The Lady Ann (family name)	Dear Lady Ann
Marquess	The Marquess of Smithshire	Dear Lord Smithshire
Marchioness	The Marchioness of Smithshire	Dear Lady Smithshire
Eldest son of marquess (usually takes his father's second title as a courtesy title)	Viscount Smithshire	Dear Lord Smithshire
Younger son / daughter of marquess	Same as younger son / daughter of duke	Same as younger son / daughter of duke
Earl	The Earl of Smithshire	Dear Lord Smithshire
Countess	The Countess of Smithshire	Dear Lady Smithshire
Eldest son of earl (usually takes his father's second title as a courtesy title)	Viscount Smithshire	Dear Lord Smithshire
Younger son of earl	The Hon. James (family name)	Dear Mr (family name)
Wife of younger son of earl	The Hon. Mrs James (family name)	Dear Mrs (family name)
Daughter of earl	The Lady Ann (family name)	Dear Lady Ann

Viscount	The Viscount Smithshire	Dear Lord Smithshire
Viscountess	The Viscountess Smithshire	Dear Lady Smithshire
Son of a viscount	The Hon. James (family name)	Dear Mr (family name)
Wife of a viscount's son	The Hon. Mrs James (family name)	Dear Mrs (family name)
Daughter of a viscount	The Hon. Anne (family name)	Dear Miss (family name)
Baron	The Lord Smith	Dear Lord Smith
Baron's wife	The Lady Smith	Dear Lady Smith
Children of baron	Same form of children of viscounts	
Baronet	Sir James Smith, Bt.	Dear Sir James
Wife of baronet	Lady Smith	Dear Lady Smith
Children of baronet	They have no titles	
Life peer	The Lord Smith of Smithshire	Dear Lord Smith
Wife of life peer	The Lady Smith of Smithshire	Dear Lady Smith
Children of life peer	The Hon. Ann / James (family name)	Dear Mr / Miss (family name)
Knight	Sir James Smith*	Dear Sir James
Knight's wife	Lady Smith	Dear Lady Smith

*Knights other than Knights Bachelor, i.e.Knights of the various Orders of Chivalry, also take postnominal letters after the name on the envelope, e.g. GCB and KCVO

117

Hereditary peeress in her own right	The Countess of Smithshire	Dear Lady Smithshire
Widow of hereditary peer	The Dowager Marchioness of Smithshire	Dear Lady Smithshire
Former wife of hereditary peer	Anne, Countess of Smithshire	Dear Lady Smithshire
Life peeress	The Baroness Smith of Smithshire	Dear Lady Smithshire
Dame	Dame Anne Smith	Dear Dame Anne
Widow of baronet	Dowager Lady Smith	Dear Lady Smith
Men	James Smith, Esq.,	Dear Mr Smith
Married Women	Mrs James Smith	Dear Mrs Smith
Unmarried women	Miss Jane Smith	Dear Miss Smith
Widows	Mrs James Smith	Dear Mrs Smith
Divorcees	Mrs Ann Smith	Dear Mrs Smith

The Prime Minister	The Rt. Hon James Smith, MP, The Prime Minister	Dear Prime Minister
The Deputy Prime Minister	The Rt. Hon. James Smith, The Deputy Prime Minister	Dear Deputy Prime Minister
The Chancellor of the Exchequer	The Rt. Hon. James Smith, The Chancellor of the Exchequer	Dear Chancellor
Lord Privy Seal	The Rt. Hon. The Earl of, The Lord Privy Seal	Dear Lord Privy Seal

The President of the Board of Trade	The Rt. Hon. The President of the Board of Trade	Dear President Dear Minister
Minister	The Rt. Hon. Sir James Smith, KBE MP, Secretary of State for ….	
Backbencher	James Smith, Esq., MP	Dear Mr Smith

The Lord Chancellor	The Rt Hon. The Lord Chancellor	
The Lord Chief Justice of England	The Rt. Hon. The Lord Chief Justice of England	
Master of the Rolls	The Rt. Hon. The Master of the Rolls	
The President of the Family Division	The Rt. Hon. The President of the Family Division	
Lords of Appeal (in Ordinary)	The Rt. Hon. The Lord Smith	
Lord Justice of the Court of Appeal	The Rt. Hon. Lord Justice Smith	
High-court judge	The Hon. Mr Justice Scribe	
Woman high-court judge	The Hon. Mrs Justice Smith, DBE	
Circuit judge	His Honour Judge Smith/ His Honour SirJames Smith	
Queen's Counsel	James Smith, Esq. QC	

Useful addresses

Smythson's:	40 New Bond Street, London W1
Wren Press:	26 Chelsea Wharf, 15 Lots Road, London SW10 0QJ. Tel: 020 7351 5887 Fax: 020 7352 7063 Website: www.wrenpress.co.uk
Piccolo Press:	90 Harbour Street, Nairn, Scotland IV12 4PG. Tel: 01667 454508 Fax: 01667 454509 Website: www.scotland-info.co.uk/piccolo
Penfriend (London) Ltd:	Bush House, Strand, London WC2B 4PH Tel: 020 7836-9809 and 34 Burlington Arcade, Piccadilly, London W1V 9AD
The Battersea Pen Home:	PO Box 4361, London SW11 4XP. Tel (020) 7652-4695 Fax (020) 7652-7338 Website: www.penhome.co.uk. Tel: (020) 7499 6337

Bibliography

Mason, Douglas, Privatizing the Posts, Adam Smith Institute, 1989
Bowie, Archibald, The Romance of the British Post Office, S W Partridge & Co, 1897
Walker, George, Haste, Post, Haste, George G Harrap & Co, 1938
Morgan, John, Debrett's New Guide to Etiquette & Modern Manners, Headline, 1996
Montague-Smith, Patrick (ed.), Debrett's Correct Form, Headline, 1970